spies

spies

THE UNDERCOVER WORLD
OF SECRETS, GADGETS
AND LIES

David Owen

Foreword by
Antonio J. Mendez
Former CIA Agent

FIREFLY BOOKS

A FIREFLY BOOK

Published by Firefly Books Ltd., 2004

Copyright © 2003 Quintet Publishing Ltd.

First Printing
National Library of Canada Cataloguing in Publication Data
Owen, David
   Spies : the undercover world of secrets, gadgets and lies / David Owen ;
foreword by Antonio J. Mendez.
Includes index.
ISBN 1-55297-795-1 (bound).—ISBN 1-55297-794-3 (pbk.)

   1. Espionage—Juvenile literature. 2. Spies—Juvenile literature. I.
Title.

UB270.5.O94 2004 j327.12 C2003-900789-8

Publisher in Cataloguing-in-Publication Data (U.S.)

Owen, David.
 Spies : the undercover world of secrets, gadgets and lies / David Owen ;
foreword by Antonio J. Mendez. – 1st ed.
[128] p. ; col. ill. : cm.
Includes index.
Summary: History of espionage, spies and spy technology, including twenty case studies.
ISBN 1-55297-795-1
ISBN 1-55297-794-3 (pbk.)
1. Spies. 2. Espionage – Equipment and supplies. I. Mendez, Antonio J. II.
Title.
327.12 21 UB270.5.O971 2004

Published in Canada in 2004 by
Firefly Books Ltd.
66 Leek Crescent
Richmond Hill, Ontario L4B 1H1

Published in the United States in 2004 by
Firefly Books (U.S.) Inc.
P.O. Box 1338, Ellicott Station
Buffalo, New York 14205

This book was designed and produced by
Quintet Publishing Limited
6 Blundell Street
London N7 7 BH

TSEC

Editor: Catherine Osborne
Text adaptation: Victoria Sherrow

Designer: James Lawrence

Creative Director: Richard Dewing
Publisher: Oliver Salzmann

Manufactured in Singapore by Universal Graphics Pte Ltd
Printed in China by Midas Printing International Ltd

Contents

YOU ARE NOW
LEAVING
BRITISH SECTOR

MIL. POLICE SIGN

FOREWORD

As one of those in the CIA who helped to defeat the enemy in that long conflict between East and West known as the Cold War, I saw firsthand that deception is, and always was, a key element in the profession of espionage. The readers of this book will learn that lesson, among others.

ABOVE Keeping terrorists from committing atrocities like the crashing of an airliner into the Pentagon on September 11, 2001, calls for high-quality intelligence.

In the world of espionage, deception means to gain strategic advantage, and that is what spies hope to achieve for the causes they represent. A professional spy needs a strong moral compass to sort out bad lies from good ones. They must not lie for personal gain but rather to protect the strategies and secrets of their cause.

The use of deception dates back millennia to early generals and soldiers. In *The Art of War,* Chinese general Sun Tzu outlined some of these tactics. In more recent decades, the imaginations of intelligence officers and the budgets of intelligence agencies like the CIA, SIS and the KGB have driven the progress of espionage technology. Any gadget introduced in a James Bond movie probably already had a counterpart in reality. Society benefits from much of this technology after it reaches the marketplace. Yet most of the public knows very little about these developments, some of which are described in this book.

Today's technical means of intelligence collection have increased the number of questions. This redoubles the need to have well-placed human sources, called agents, working in place with access

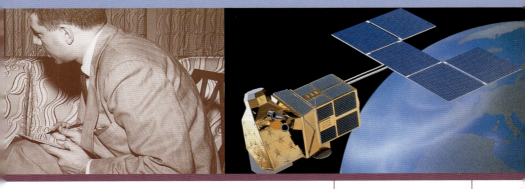

to the enemy's secrets. They can provide insights about the opponent's thoughts and intentions that intelligence collected by other means cannot.

When agents gain access to a secret, they must protect it with their lives. Intelligence services strive to keep their agents in place and alive as long as possible, to maintain timely and secure communications, and to get them out when their time is up. The means used to maintain secure operations is known as tradecraft. Some of the tradecraft still used is based on techniques from the beginning of time. As a career technical operations officer in CIA, my colleagues and I were responsible for creating and deploying many of the forms of technical tradecraft — the gadgets that keep our agents secure.

Disguise and illusion go hand in hand with deception. They are more about how we must manage the operational stage, to figure out the enemy's point of view, and exactly who is the audience we are trying to fool, including their expectations and limitations. Then we must present them with an idea so they can follow it while we are simultaneously hiding the real purpose and action in the deception. These principles are illustrated in some of the case studies in this book.

Some spies were the most honorable of the great unsung heroes and others were motivated to deceive for selfish reasons or a failed cause. Often right and wrong depends on a person's point of view. But as was said before, a strong moral compass helps when navigating the dark terrain of the spy's world.

Antonio J. Mendez
Former Intelligence Officer, August 2001

THE BEGINNINGS OF ESPIONAGE

Secret codes ... hidden cameras and recorders ... stolen microfilm ... exploding pens ... a lone agent veiled in shadows. These images come to mind when we think about espionage — acts designed to steal the ideas, plans or capabilities of an enemy or possible enemy. Since ancient times, soldiers have wondered: What lies over the hill? Where are the enemy's strongholds? Are they hiding men or *matériel*? Do they have any weakness that could be used to defeat them? Exposing these secrets can change the outcome of a battle or shorten a war campaign and save lives.

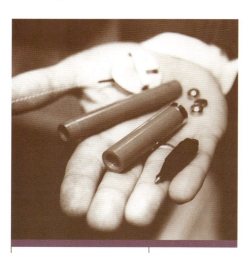

ABOVE Hollow pen shaft used to hide and transport papers and codes.

Spies are also vital in times of political tension rather than war. Knowing an adversary's true bargaining position can give one side a huge advantage when signing treaties or settling claims over disputed territory. At times, military leaders have decided to launch attacks after finding out secrets that showed the enemy was weak. Espionage can help make the world safer. During the Cold War, a show of power was important. Both East and West had to know each nation could destroy the other. That way, neither would want to press the nuclear button.

Yet, when it comes to gathering human intelligence, who is the real spymaster? Is the agent who returns from enemy country really telling you what you need to know — or what your adversary wants you to think? Even when people rely on electronic intelligence rather than personal

accounts, their opponents can give them false information. The double-edged nature of espionage makes this high-stakes activity even more fascinating. The use of double, triple or even multiple agents can create confusion and keep people guessing. If an agent might be working for the other side, why not trick his or her "employer"? Instead of catching the agent and cutting off that line of communication, you can feed a double agent false information and give the enemy a false sense of security. In reality, the spy takes them information that you want them to believe and brings back planted information that can show what secrets the enemy wants to hide. Without realizing it, the double agent has become a triple agent. The true value of the information has switched to the other side.

ABOVE The forged Argentinian identity papers of Nazi official Adolf Eichmann that allowed him to evade capture and trial.

Clearly, spying involves more than simply seeking and then passing on information. And the human cost can be terribly high. A spy can be exposed at any time. Capture could mean a long prison sentence or even execution. To avoid detection, spies must trust no one and must learn to live completely "undercover." They give up the normal rewards of career, family life and friendships, except under carefully controlled circumstances. Even after they retire, agents may continue to make compromises. Usually the host country is not their homeland, since agents tend to spy in their native societies, where they can blend in undetected. The country for which

ABOVE Francis Gary Powers under trial by the USSR Supreme Court's Military Collegium (see Case Study 15).

they operate is often an alien society, where the customs and language are different. This makes it hard for them to return to a normal civilian life.

Although technology now reveals many secrets, individual agents still play a vital role. Humans can provide data that mechanical systems would not pick up. These include the goals of a nation's leaders in a particular campaign or crisis, the existence of dissident groups or individuals who could be recruited as agents, and shifts in public attitudes that may be important in tense political times. Nevertheless, traditional spies operate in a vastly more complex world than the spies of earlier times. Intelligence information is assembled from many sources, including signal intelligence (obtained from the interception and decrypting of messages, and the analysis of traffic), electronic intelligence (involving remote sensors and traffic surveillance) and image intelligence (including video intelligence and airborne information gathering).

This book covers various aspects of intelligence and information gathering, including the methods countries and their counterintelligence organizations use to guard their secrets. Today's world features a greater number of less powerful potential adversaries, so agents may go back to some of the espionage traditions of the past. The world of twenty-first century espionage is challenging and so far largely unpredictable. Yet, revealing the hidden secrets of tomorrow will certainly continue to engage the brightest and the bravest, as agents match wits with those who doggedly guard those secrets. The future of this ancient profession promises to be just as busy and colorful as the past.

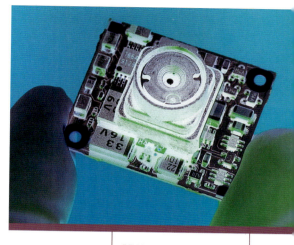

ABOVE Modern electronics have changed espionage technology: This miniature video camera is ideal for covert surveillance in homes or offices, and can be connected to standard television and video monitors for playing back the results.

LEFT This artificial stone, made in Poland during the 1980s, has a hollowed center in which agents can leave messages without attracting attention.

1

SPYING ON THE ENEMY

In times of war a nation's survival can hinge on the work of its secret agents. The valuable information they uncover can often provide the vital key needed to defeat the enemy. Equally, agents also maintain a nation's security during peacetime. This was particularly true during the turbulent twentieth century where agents monitored threats and reassured countries that they need not fear an attack.

Both "superpowers" — the US and Soviet Union — built strong organizations. Russia's long tradition of espionage dated back to the sixteenth century, when the paranoid Ivan the Terrible used spies. In the early 1900s, the first secret police organization, the Tsarist Ochrana, spied on Russian citizens to spot signs of dissent or revolution. Ochrana agents joined dissident groups and also tried to lure other

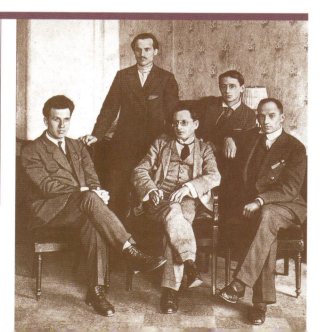

RIGHT The directors of the Communist Cheka secret police organization set up its Moscow headquarters in 1918 to replace the Tsarist Ochrana, whose teams of undercover agents (OPPOSITE TOP) had watched every level of Russian society.

members into taking risky actions that could lead to their arrest and exile in Siberia.

In the Russian Revolution of 1917, the Bolsheviks overthrew Nicholas II and seized power. Lenin's new regime simply replaced the Ochrana with the Cheka (the Extraordinary Commission for Combating Counterrevolution and Sabotage), the precursor of the KGB (Soviet State Security Committee). The fledgling Communist state launched a major espionage effort to combat threats from outside and within. Through the years, its focus changed. Between the world wars, Russian espionage mainly worked to undermine anti-Communist groups that had taken refuge overseas; many agents were recruited from the Communist parties in those target nations. After World War II, the devastation caused by the German invasion led the Russians to fear more possible invasions from the West.

Chasing Atomic Secrets

When the US dropped atomic bombs over Hiroshima and Nagasaki in 1945, forcing the Japanese to surrender, the Russians felt quite vulnerable, despite their vast armed forces and huge territory. Eager to possess the same power, they relentlessly dug out the secrets of this awesome

BELOW The aftermath of the nuclear bomb attack on Hiroshima and Nagasaki.

new weapon and successfully tested their own atomic bombs in 1949, while continuing to spy on the West. Alarmed, Western intelligence redoubled their own efforts within the Communist bloc.

President Harry Truman shut down the OSS (Office of Strategic Services — a network of US agents that spied on Nazi Germany) in 1945, saying it had no place in the new peacetime world. But Russia's aggressive tactics convinced him to set up a new organization, the Central Intelligence Agency (CIA), under the control of the National Security Council (NSC) and linking the intelligence arms of the three armed service branches. Based in Langley, Virginia, the CIA gained a first-rate reputation, even though the US had little experience with espionage.

ABOVE US President Harry S Truman made the decision to drop nuclear bombs on Hiroshima and Nagasaki.

OPPOSITE TOP Gehlen's chief of counter-intelligence, Heinz Felfe, was revealed to be a Russian double agent.

RIGHT The early structure crosses the middle of a street as the Berlin wall goes up.

The Gehlen Bureau

The West boosted its network by hiring seasoned professionals. They included Reinhard Gehlen, a former army officer who directed a key branch of German military intelligence on the Russians during World War II. His agents gained detailed knowledge of Russian strengths, weapons and capabilities.

As the war was ending, Lieutenant General Gehlen prepared microfilm copies of all his records and destroyed the originals. When Gehlen surrendered, he offered his captors vast quantities of information on the Soviets — and the US accepted. In 1955, he switched employers, to head the intelligence service for the new Federal Republic of West Germany. There, he produced valuable information on Communist East Germany. His agents included a member of the East German Cabinet and an employee for East German Intelligence.

But even Gehlen had his failures. His agents gave him no advance warning that the Soviets would close the East-West border in Berlin in 1961 and build the Berlin Wall. Later that year, he suffered a severe blow upon learning that his own chief of counterintelligence, Heinz Felfe, had been a spy for the Russians for over 10 years!

Israeli Intelligence

While East-West espionage efforts focused on the opposition's strengths, intentions and nuclear secrets, other countries had different priorities. One of the best is Mossad, the Israeli external espionage organization, which also deals with domestic issues. Its Special Operations Department carries out actions against those who may threaten the state, and to punish its enemies. In 1960, Mossad agents went to Argentina and arrested Adolf Eichmann, the notorious Nazi official who had arranged for the transportation of European Jews to Hitler's death camps during World War II.

ABOVE Nazi official Adolf Eichmann lived after the war in Argentina on forged identity papers and was seized by Israeli agents in **1960** to be put on trial for his role in the systematic murder of European Jews.

Mossad also hunted for, and assassinated, the Arab terrorists who murdered Israeli athletes at the 1972 Olympic Games in Munich. When an Israeli aircraft was hijacked to Entebbe in Uganda in 1976, the Israelis mounted a long-distance raid that freed the captives.

Great Spies of the American Revolution

Today's world of spying often relies on hi-tech tools, but great spies from the past found clever ways to outwit their enemies. During the American Revolution, when the American colonies won their independence from England, one of General George Washington's top spies was the double agent Sergeant John Honeyman, who had fought with him in the British Army. Honeyman supplied information that enabled the Americans to cross the Delaware River and capture Trenton in the fierce winter of 1776. This victory lifted morale and turned the tide at a time when the American cause seemed doomed after a string of defeats, combined with hunger, bad weather and scarce supplies.

In 1780, New York was the headquarters and chief base for British forces. Washington's intelligence chief, Colonel Benjamin Tallmadge, maintained a network of spies within the city. The Culper Ring recruited traders and craftsmen who worked for the British Army. They sent vital information to Washington's headquarters using their secret weapon: invisible ink. In fact, loyalties crossed the fighting lines in both directions. One of Britain's top agents was none other than American General Benedict Arnold, while Edward Bancroft, secretary to Benjamin Franklin in Paris, was reporting directly to London. Even so, Washington was able to score another dramatic coup against the British after his spies warned that the enemy planned to use naval support against rebel

BELOW Washington crosses the Delaware at the head of his retreating army at a moment of great peril for the American cause.

forces around Newport, Rhode Island. Washington seized the opportunity to send a double agent, who falsely reported that the Americans would attack New York itself. In truth, Washington's forces were far too weak to carry out that action. But the British commander trusted the information from this apparently reliable source and chose to retreat within New York's defenses. As a result, Washington's French allies landed safely at Newport.

Secret Ink

Invisible ink could be revealed by warming the paper or brushing it with the right chemical. The earliest types of invisible ink, like sugar solution, milk or lemon juice, reappear when heated. Messages written with copper sulphate can be read by brushing with a chemical solution of sodium iodide.

Eighteenth-century spies had a tough time passing information through a war-torn country. They relied on invisible ink and wrote between the lines of otherwise innocent papers. For example, the Culper Ring used a preparation called Jay's Sympathetic Stain to relay vital information to George Washington's headquarters. As the ink dried, the message disappeared. It only reappeared when brushed with the right reagent.

In the summer of 1780, the Culper Ring learned that the British planned to send troops from New York to Newport. They sent this information to General Washington, using Sympathetic Stain ink on the back of an ordinary business letter to a colonel in Brookhaven.

After Washington read the hidden message, he quickly wrote a letter describing a massive attack on New York. A double agent passed this on to the British. After reading the false letter, the British ordered Clinton's forces to return, while the fleet sailed back to New York, allowing French troops to land unopposed.

LEFT Washington watches his men crossing the Delaware river to win a vital respite from the British pursuit.

Tricks of the Trade

Since ancient times, spies have risked their lives to obtain information, then copy it or smuggle it out of its original setting or across a border. Detection could bring disaster to both the individual and the network. To survive, an agent must master what the intelligence services call their tradecraft. This includes basic skills, like a strong cover story, and details, like the methods they use to pass information and contact their superiors. They must be able to tell if they are being trailed and, if so, shake off their pursuers. Information can be passed on in different ways. Often, they will set up an apparently casual meeting to transfer a note or roll of film from agent to supporter. Such meetings can be prearranged by a secret message or by leaving a sign on an agreed landmark, like a chalked mark on a streetlight. Sometimes "dead drops" are used: the agent simply leaves the material in an innocuous place; a supporter retrieves it after spotting the prearranged warning mark.

Over the years, technology has helped to make a spy's work easier and a bit safer. The invention of the microdot makes it possible to reduce a

BELOW Espionage equipment, including briefcases with a hidden videocamera and tape recorder and tape recorders hidden in cigarette packs and wristwatches.

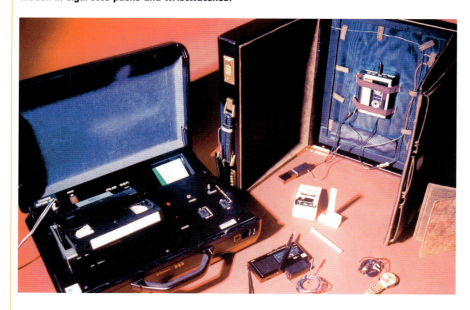

**ABOVE Radio transmitting
and receiving equipment.**

page of information to the size of a period on a printed page. Now, a mass
of data can be hidden under a postage stamp, or as part of a typed letter,
then sent through the regular mail. Also, the advent of the compact
cellular phone has made it much easier for teams of shadowers to track a
potentially elusive subject.

A successful agent must blend into the host society as perfectly as
possible. Even trivial details may reveal an impostor. During World War II,
German spies in Britain were frequently Irishmen. They spoke English well,
but their ignorance of wartime regulations caused them to be reported to
the authorities. One spy exposed himself by asking for a drink at an inn
during the afternoon, when the liquor laws banned this request; another
asked for a whiskey at a bar where this drink had been unobtainable for
months. Strangers in quiet rural communities were quickly suspect,
especially when their clothes looked foreign-made. To guard against such
problems, Britain's Special Operations Executive insisted that, among
other things, his spies have their British dental work remade in
Continental style before they were dropped into Occupied Europe.

True or False?

The information that spies gather obviously varies in importance, and a spy may not even realize its full meaning. Small details may determine the overall intelligence picture, especially in wartime, when people are not able to travel within the target country. This was certainly true in the twentieth century. During World War II, British intelligence cleverly figured out how references to German weapons research at Peenemünde, on the Baltic coast, were genuine, and not planted to fool the Allies. An independent source of information showed that the Germans were making certain that Peenemünde received gas and oil supplies. The British agent, whose name was Jones, reasoned that if the Germans were laying a false trail, they would not cover their tracks that much. He urged the Allies to investigate Peenemünde further.

If British intelligence had lacked this evidence or thought the story was fake, the agent's brave work would have been wasted and the Germans might have developed war-winning weapons. Instead, the Allies investigated what scientists were doing in that remote research facility, then tried to stop them by bombing the laboratories and the employees' homes. At the very least, the Allies were not totally shocked

BELOW The first ballistic missile, the V2 rocket, being raised to its vertical firing position aboard a mobile launcher.

by the onslaught of German V1 cruise missiles and V2 ballistic rockets.

Sometimes agents provide worthwhile information, but their operators may not use it to their advantage. This happened on the eve of World War I, when the Germans received information that could have led them to victory. An Austrian agent, Baron August Schluga, sent the Germans an espionage "gem" — the entire mobilization plan for the French Army and, even better, Plan 17, the strategic thinking of Marshal Joffre, France's military commander in chief. The German commanders could hardly believe their luck, but in the end, they chose not to believe the information, fearing that the French had foisted it on Schluga to mislead them. Overcaution led them to throw away a priceless strategic advantage.

Is the information true or false? This question constantly challenged those who directed spies and spy networks during the two world wars of the twentieth century. The established espionage organizations in Germany, Austria, Russia, France and Britain worked to uncover vital secrets from their adversaries during World War I. The US joined the conflict in 1917, but had no espionage presence in Europe, where the decisive battles were being fought and where US troops were starting to fight. However, in the even more widespread campaigns of World War II, the United States realized espionage was a vital weapon. In tackling Nazi Germany through the efforts of the OSS, the US was laying the foundations for the CIA and the National Security Agency (NSA), those giants of Cold War espionage.

BELOW US President Woodrow Wilson featured on the cover of a French magazine in February 1917, just weeks before he requested a declaration of war from Congress to bring America into World War I.

PRÉSIDENT DE LA RÉPUBLIQUE DES ÉTATS-UNIS

Mutual-Assured-Destruction

Nineteen forty five heralded the beginning of the Cold War, unleashing a political culture of fear and paranoia between East and West that would last until the Soviet Union collapsed in December 1991. Although there was no actual warfare, the US and Russia had enough nuclear weaponry to destroy the world. At the flick of a switch nuclear war could become a scary reality. Each side knew the other could retaliate with nuclear weapons. This was the doctrine of MAD — Mutual Assured Destruction: deterrence based on the knowledge that each side could destroy the other if attacked.

On the other hand, each side wanted to know what kinds of nuclear forces its adversary had developed and where they were located. This knowledge could reduce the threat and tilt the balance of power. Espionage services working for the NATO (North Atlantic Treaty Organization) and Warsaw Pact countries continued to seek this kind of information right through to the 1990s, when the US embarked on its new "Star Wars" antimissile defense systems. The Soviets faced an arms race they clearly could not win, and the East-West balance collapsed rather quickly. The Soviet frontiers diminished, and the Warsaw Pact countries adopted neutral status or signed up with NATO.

Espionage, however, remained just as popular after the Cold War ended. But the priorities were not as clear-cut and the threats seemed much more hazy and complex. Weapons of mass destruction now include chemical and biological as well as nuclear. They are easier to hide and deliver than ever before. And terrorism and religious fundamentalism have joined ideology and power politics as reasons to keep a close eye on one's allies, neighbors, trading partners and competitors as well as opponents.

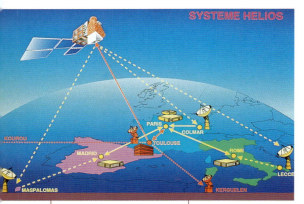

ABOVE Diagram of the range and capability of *Helios*, the first European defense satellite.

OPPOSITE Characteristic nuclear explosion mushroom cloud that has been an image of terror for generations.

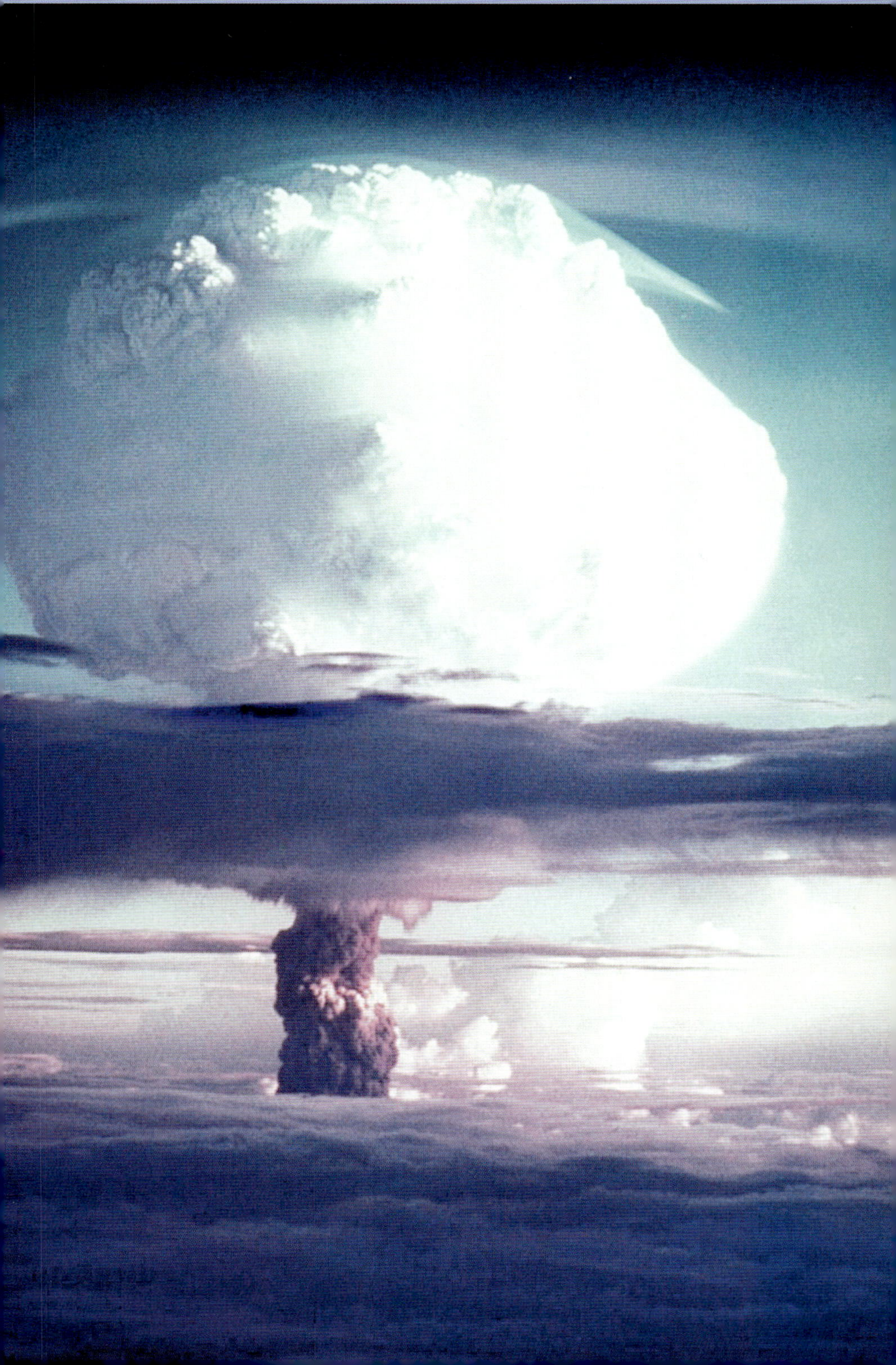

THE FRENCH PAINTER

OCCUPIED FRANCE, 1943

By 1943, it was clear the Allies would attempt a landing in Nazi-occupied Europe. The Germans were fortifying the entire coast with bunkers, gun emplacements and minefields. The Allies needed to know as much as possible about these defenses. What they needed were the German's plans — but that was hardly possible.

However, on May 7, a French decorator and resistance agent named René Duchez spotted an official notice at Caen in Normandy. The Todt Organization, the German body responsible for building the defenses, was inviting bids from decorators to repair and redecorate its local offices.

BELOW Detailed maps of the German defenses along the Western side of the Cotentin peninsula in Normandy were based on reports from agents in occupied France.

Duchez seized the opportunity. He quoted a price one-third less than the true cost and was told to come back the next day. While he was at Todt conferring with Bauleiter Schnedderer, the head of the Caen

office, an assistant brought in a pile of maps. To Duchez's astonishment, one of them was a master map that showed all the fortifications planned for the Normandy coast. Hiding his excitement, he continued discussing wallpaper, while the maps remained on the desk.

After Schnedderer briefly left his office, Duchez moved quickly. He hid the map behind a wall mirror, hoping he could whisk it away later. He ignored the other maps, trusting that the Germans would not notice one missing. When Schnedderer returned, they picked a pattern, and Duchez agreed to start on the following Monday.

After a nervous weekend, the courageous Duchez returned to Todt, hoping to retrieve the map. But Schnedderer was gone. He had been replaced by Bauleiter Keller, who insisted that the work contract did not cover his own office. Thinking fast, Duchez explained that he had agreed to include that room in his price, in return for future jobs.

The Germans were delighted with their "bargain." When Duchez finished his work at Todt, he met some fellow resistance members at a café. A German captain was sitting nearby, so he could not mention the map. A chilling moment occurred when a Gestapo car pulled into the square. But it soon passed on.

When the captain stood up to leave, Duchez reached for the German's overcoat and helped him put it on. Afterwards, the others asked Duchez what he would have done if the Gestapo had come inside to search the café. Duchez smiled and explained that, as a precaution, he had hidden the map in the German's coat pocket, then pulled it back out when the captain was leaving.

BELOW Hitler meeting representatives of the Todt Organization, responsible for planning and building the fortifications along the French coast, designed to repel any landings.

SUCCESS ON THE WARFRONT
SWITZERLAND AND GERMANY, 1942–45

Although the British had major problems setting up a network of spies in Nazi Germany, the Americans had better luck. The forerunner to both the OSS and the CIA was the innocent-sounding Office of the Coordinator of Information, set up by President Roosevelt in 1941. In June 1942, the organization was renamed the OSS (Office of Strategic Services). That November, American Allen Dulles traveled by train through Vichy, France, to Berne, Switzerland, carrying a letter of credit for a million dollars, to set up an OSS forward office close to Germany. His cover role was "special legal assistant to the American Minister to Switzerland." But word soon spread through the espionage underworld that the OSS was open for business.

Several would-be informers contacted Dulles's office, but the information they offered seemed doubtful when compared with data the OSS had received through "Ultra" (see Chapter 2) and other forms of communications intelligence. More promising information arrived in August 1943 when Fritz Kolbe, a German courier, showed Dulles copies of German Foreign Office cables. Kolbe promised to bring more when he returned to Switzerland.

The OSS faced a crucial decision. Was the information false, perhaps sent deliberately by the Germans' own spy services? Dulles knew the risks of trusting the information: if he passed copies to London or Washington by radio, German counterespionage agents might be able to break the codes. They might also have enough evidence to have the OSS thrown out of Berne for violating Swiss neutrality.

Nevertheless, the information was very convincing, and fit what was known through "Ultra" and other sources. Kolbe gave Dulles a wealth of personal information, which the Americans could check for themselves. On October 7, 1943, he delivered more than 200 pages of messages. He returned three more times with over 1,600 documents, including many secret dispatches from German military attachés overseas. This priceless information included details of Spanish dictator Franco's plot to smuggle tungsten to Germany's steel industries in crates of oranges and of a German radio station in neutral Ireland that reported on Allied shipping movements. Both operations were stopped after protests from the Allies.

Kolbe also revealed that the Albanian valet to the British ambassador to Turkey was a spy who stole documents from his employer's safe for the Germans. The documents included the top-secret plans for the invasion of Europe. The Germans suspected that the British had planted this information, so they did not act on it!

Other OSS operations managed to penetrate close to the heart of Hitler's Germany. Dulles ran eight networks in Occupied France that relayed key details of German targets to be attacked leading up to the D-Day landings, while German agents brought information on the development of V1 and V2 weapons at Peenemünde. In the summer of 1944, the OSS took the offensive: 50 two-man teams, supplied by de Gaulle's intelligence service, were parachuted into France to report on German troop movements at the time of the invasion. Thirty-four teams of OSS agents were also dropped into Germany, under the authority of future CIA director William Casey. Four of the most successful agents radio-ed back to specially equipped aircraft flying over Germany by night, giving details of rail routes, troop movements and potential targets.

ABOVE Allen Dulles, wartime head of the American Office of Strategic Services (OSS) branch in Switzerland from November 1942.

OPPOSITE William Casey ran the program involving OSS agents in Germany and later directed the OSS's successor, the CIA.

STEALING ATOMIC SECRETS
US AND UK, 1940s

On June 3, 1945, Harry Gold, a chemist from Philadelphia, arrived at the home of David and Ruth Greenglass in Albuquerque, New Mexico. The two men identified themselves by "matching up" two cut halves of a cardboard panel from a carton of raspberry jello. Then Greenglass accepted $500 in cash. In return, he handed Gold some notes and sketches, which Gold placed in a large manila envelope. Gold carried another manila envelope in a folded newspaper. It contained some notes he had received the day before, in Santa Fe, from a German-born British scientist, Dr Klaus Fuchs.

After leaving the Greenglass home, Gold headed to New York, where he met with Anatoly Yakovlev, a clerk from the Russian Embassy. They exchanged newspapers before walking away in opposite directions. The newspaper Gold received was empty. But Yakovlev left with enough information to give Russia a head start in making its own atomic bomb, saving years of expensive development work.

BELOW Dr Klaus Emil Fuchs, German-born physicist and spy (center), is led away from Heathrow airport in London under police escort.

OPPOSITE BOTTOM The Russian spy Harry Gold, after being arrested by two United States Deputy Marshals.

In the USSR, Stalin knew about efforts to build atomic weapons. Since it would take decades of work to catch up with the West, the Soviets had resolved to steal those priceless secrets. Aided by Communist sympathizers, Russian espionage had begun in the US while the bomb was being made. Yakovlev's

network included Julius and Ethel Rosenberg; Julius worked for the US Signal Corps during the war. In 1944, Ethel's brother, David Greenglass, was assigned to the Manhattan Project, the code name for the bomb-building project. He sold vital technical details for cash.

As part of the network, Klaus Fuchs had passed information to the Russians while conducting nuclear research in England. Transferred to the Manhattan Project in 1943, he began supplying details of American work on the bomb. Alan Nunn May, a British physicist working on nuclear research in Canada, also gave the Russians information, based on the briefings he received in the US.

ABOVE David Greenglass, shown here escorted by a US Deputy Marshal, passed on nuclear bomb information to the Russians for cash.

On September 23, 1949, the work of these spies became obvious when the Soviets conducted a nuclear test explosion deep in their heartland. The West saw that its former ally had stolen their atomic secrets and was showing increasing hostility.

The West soon got revenge, however. A cipher clerk who defected from the Soviet Embassy in Ottawa in September 1945 gave evidence that Nunn May was a spy. May was arrested, tried and imprisoned. With information from the Canadians, the FBI (Federal Bureau of Investigation) and British intelligence unmasked Klaus Fuchs, who had returned to England in 1946 and was working for the UK Atomic Energy Research Establishment. Fuchs was arrested and gave information that led to the arrest of Gold, Greenglass and, ultimately, to the Rosenbergs. Gold, Fuchs and Greenglass received prison sentences, but the Rosenbergs, who were portrayed as the ringleaders in the conspiracy, were sentenced to death in 1953 despite a vast international outcry to spare their lives.

A BRAVE DOUBLE AGENT

RUSSIA, 1961–62

Some Russians took enormous risks to spy for the West. One of the most successful was Colonel Oleg Penkovskiy, a war hero who had worked for Russian military intelligence during the 1950s. By 1959, he was deeply worried that Khrushchev's leadership might trigger a world war. To help prevent this, he began to collaborate with the West.

ABOVE Presented with evidence which included spy cameras and rolls of film and coded writings on postcards, the judges at the Penkovskiy and Wynne trials found both men guilty of espionage.

In April 1961, Penkovskiy approached Greville Wynne, a British businessman who was in Moscow making plans for a Russian trade delegation's visit to the UK, which Penkovskiy would lead. Wynne himself had been involved in intelligence work, and he agreed to talk with the right people in London. When the Russian delegation arrived there, Penkovskiy met with representatives of the British and American intelligence agencies, who decided he was sincere. He seized every opportunity during his visit to give information to Western controllers. Communications were set up and he agreed to send back more information after he returned to Moscow.

When Wynne next visited Moscow, Penkovskiy handed him 20 rolls of film, covering everything from operating manuals for missiles to Russian intelligence documents. Later that year, Penkovskiy supplied more information. He also took back material provided by his Western contacts, to convince his Soviet masters that he was spying on the West.

Colonel Oleg Penkovskiy

In Moscow, as Penkovskiy continued passing material to different contacts, he sensed that he was being "shadowed." He made use of different methods, such as "dead drops," or signaling his contacts by making a black mark on a certain streetlight, or by letting a phone ring for a set number of times.

However, the KGB remained suspicious. By July 1962, Penkovskiy knew he was being watched and realized the KGB also suspected Wynne. When the two men met at the restaurant that week, Penkovskiy's trained eye spotted some KGB agents. He left immediately and waited outside for Wynne.

ABOVE Oleg Penkovskiy at the opening of his trial in Moscow's Soviet Supreme Court.

BELOW A year after Oleg Penkovskiy was sentenced to death, Greville Wynne (shown with his wife) was released in exchange for Soviet agent Gordon Lonsdale.

They risked only a few brief words. Wynne was due to fly out of Moscow the next morning, and Penkovskiy promised to see him off. Returning to his office, he made a formal complaint against the KGB surveillance, since he had reported Wynne as a contact who could help the Soviets, as a cover story to explain their meetings. The KGB apologized. But Wynne remained worried. He and Penkovskiy decided Wynne would change his afternoon flight to leave around 9 p.m. instead. Wynne departed safely, and it seemed that the KGB had been outwitted.

But they had the last word. After Penkovskiy handed the West the details of Russian missiles (which enabled American reconnaissance to identify the missile types the Russians installed in Cuba during the subsequent missile crisis), the KGB arrested him on October 22, 1962. Eleven days later, Wynne was arrested while setting up a trade exhibition in Budapest, Hungary. The two men next met in Moscow's dreaded Lubyanka prison. At their trials in 1963, both were found guilty of espionage. Penkovskiy was shot, while Wynne was imprisoned. A year later, he was exchanged for a KGB colonel who had been captured in the UK.

CODE BREAKING

A secret message is useless if the enemy can find it and figure out what it means. Since ancient times, spies have looked for newer and better ways to hide messages. Cryptology — creating different systems to represent the letters of a message with other letters — was developed to baffle those who did not know the system. In response, people developed the art of decrypting.

RIGHT Leon Battista Alberti, Florentine inventor of the cipher wheel.

OPPOSITE TOP Early cipher wheel that uses revolving disks that can be aligned in different ways to encipher and decipher text.

OPPOSITE RIGHT This World War II German Enigma cipher machine has four rotors, of the type issued to the German Navy, making its messages more difficult to break than those sent by Army and Luftwaffe three-rotor machines.

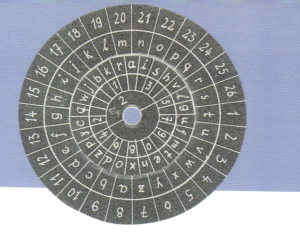

Cipher Devices

To help people write and decipher messages, spies and diplomats began using mechanical devices. An early example is the cipher wheel, invented by Leon Battista Alberti, an Italian cryptologist, in the late fifteenth century. The 26 letters of the alphabet were arranged in random order around the edge of a disk. In turn, it was pinned to the center of a larger disk which also had the 26 letters around its rim. The two disks were free to rotate relative to one another. To encipher a message, the disks were rotated so that a letter on the inner disk lined up with a different letter on the outer disk. This pairing would be revealed in the first letters of the message, say "Bj," meaning that "B" on the outer disk should be set opposite "j" on the inner disk. The writer composed the text by referring from one disk to the other.

In 1918, this early form of the cipher wheel was replaced with Arthur Scherbius's ingenious Enigma machine. Scherbuis based his invention on a normal typewriter, which he modified so that striking a key turned a disk-shaped rotor carrying 26 electrical contacts, one for each letter of the alphabet. As the typist struck each key of the plain text message, the rotor would continue to turn, bringing different contacts in touch with the machine's internal wiring. The characters were shown on paper.

Later versions displayed each character of the cipher text by lighting up one of 26 lamps on the top of the machine, each indicating a letter of the alphabet. The position of the rotor determined which lamp lit up. Since this changed as each key was

pressed, the relationship between the plain text and cipher text altered with each character typed. If the same letter was typed several times, for example, the cipher text would show a different character each time — very effective, since it amounted to using a different cipher alphabet for each letter.

Scherbius also proposed a set of rotors that would work in series, like the changing figures on a vehicle's mileage recorder. As each of the three rotors completed a full revolution, gearing would advance to the next rotor. Using three rotors increased the number of characters in a message before the original relationship was repeated to a total of 26 x 26 x 26, or 17,576. Later, a fourth rotor was added, although this did not actually turn and it had 13 contacts instead of the normal 26. This new rotor made the system even more complex.

Clearly, the recipient of this kind of message had to know the starting positions of the rotors before the first key was pressed, as well as the order in which the removable rotors were fitted into the machine. With different internal wiring, the rotors were not simply interchangeable, which would have been a potential weakness. A receiving operator

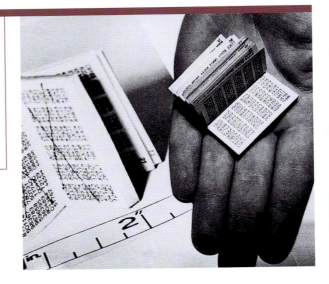

RIGHT These miniature code-books of one time pads offer even greater security than the most complex cipher machines but take time to distribute and may be captured by enemy agents.

could then set up the machine and type in the ciphered text as received by radio.

After World War I, the Germans knew the British had captured their code-books and made good use of that information. With the Enigma machine, there were no code-books. Even if a machine was seized, it would be useless without details of the rotor settings.

Furthermore, the German Navy and Army adopted versions that included a selection of rotors, all with different wiring. To decipher messages, the enemy would have to choose the correct three rotors, as well as know the settings. Later, the Army added another layer of complexity: a plugboard containing 26 sockets, which could be connected in pairs using a series of short cables. The connections were also needed to decipher Enigma machine messages.

The Germans were convinced no enemy could read messages using Enigma or crack the system. Even when the Allies showed signs they knew military plans that had been detailed in Enigma signals, the Germans refused to believe the system was flawed. Ironically, in trying to keep the British from repeating their code-breaking successes of World War I, the Germans handed their enemies a more valuable, and even more damaging, victory.

The Germans offered the Enigma system to their Japanese allies, who used the same principle for important diplomatic messages, together with the characters of the Western alphabet. However, their Alphabetical Typewriter actually printed out the cipher text using a second machine connected to the plugboard of the first. Like the Germans, the Japanese assumed their system was foolproof. But just as the British broke Enigma messages to produce a flood of key information, the Americans achieved the same success against the Japanese, and radically changed the course of the war in the Pacific.

ABOVE Two of the rotors used on an Enigma machine showing the electrical contacts between adjacent rotors which added to the complexity of the cipher. These rotors became prize catches for any interceptors of German navy craft.

ABOVE Painting from a Greek vase showing soldiers putting on their armor before one of the succession of battles between rival city states.

RIGHT The Spartans used skytale batons to conceal messages written on a parchment strip.

Sending Messages in Earlier Times

In Classical Greece, Sparta built a powerful army. They needed effective methods for sending secret information between agents and military generals. To thwart their rivals, they invented the "skytale" — a standard baton wrapped with a strip of papyrus, leather or parchment. A message was written on the wrapping, then the strip was removed and passed to the messenger. Unwound, the strip looked like a random and meaningless set of letters. The message could be deciphered when it was rewound around a baton of the same diameter.

The Romans used spies and secret ciphers. Julius Caesar encoded his letters by shifting the letters three places along in the alphabet. Later, the Arabs carried out the first logical study of how to break ciphers. To decode a hidden message, they studied the frequency with which standard letters appeared in any piece of writing in a specific language.

During the late fifteenth century, Venice created its shadowy and sinister Council of Ten to maintain its control over the Eastern Mediterranean. This group ran a large secret police force, with agents and contacts reporting from within the republic's major competitors. After being appointed in 1506, the Council's cipher secretary, Giovanni Soro, proved adept at deciphering coded messages seized by their own secret agents. His efforts were so successful that the Council regularly changed its own secret ciphers to prevent Venetian messages from being read.

Spies in Elizabethan England were used to expose plots against the monarch. In 1586, a former page of Mary, Queen of Scots, Anthony Babington, planned to kill Elizabeth and restore Roman Catholicism as the official religion, with Mary as queen. The conspirators smuggled coded letters into the house where Mary was imprisoned by hiding them in beer barrels. But Babington did not know that his own messenger, Gilbery Gifford, was a double agent working for Elizabeth. One message showed that Mary supported the assassination and an invasion by her ally, King Philip of Spain. Within weeks, Babington and his collaborators had been caught. They were beheaded, as was Mary herself.

Radio: Scrambling and Unscrambling Messages

The invention of radio during the late 1800s and early 1900s allowed people to send messages across long distances without the risk of falling into enemy hands if an agent was captured. However, anyone else with a radio receiver could intercept the messages. Only a really secure cipher would outwit a determined enemy.

Clever eavesdroppers got around the system. Because a particular radio frequency was shared, messages needed call signs to identify the sender and intended recipient. These had to be clear enough to be recognized without requiring someone to try to decrypt all the signals on a given frequency. Eavesdroppers used them as clues to help break a series of messages. Spies could also use various technical devices, such as direction finders, to pick up the location of the transmitter itself. That information could help them determine who operated that transmitter. In some cases, it gave them the opportunity to seize enemy ciphers and code-books, which they used to decipher their radio messages.

In crowded urban areas, a favorite trick was to cut off the electric power in different zones and note when a particular transmission was interrupted. In the countryside or the suburbs, an antenna could

RIGHT A typical 1940s radio receiver with its bulky cabinet and large turning dial.

pinpoint the location of a transmitter. However, as radios were made smaller and more compact, agents could carry them to places where they could spot any approaching enemy squads in advance. Radios powered by batteries were less vulnerable to interruptions in electricity supply.

Speech communication can be scrambled. Passing the signal through circuits that alter the frequency of different tones in the speaker's voice can change low frequencies to high frequencies and vice versa. The resulting noises are quite unintelligible. Different types of scrambler systems create still more confusion for eavesdroppers. Sophisticated systems can change the scrambling procedure at intervals of fractions of a second and even allow successive segments of the message to be shuffled in time order. Still another system causes the frequencies to fluctuate quickly up and down. The wartime telephone conversations between President Roosevelt and Prime Minister Churchill were also switched between different channels. Anyone listening on one particular channel would find that the signal died periodically.

Nevertheless, in September 1941, months of effort paid off when German engineers succeeded in unscrambling the signals. This meant they could listen to conversations between the two Allied leaders. In early 1944, they heard remarks about the level of military activity in Britain suggesting that the Allies would soon cross the English Channel and move into France. Shortly after that, the system was replaced by an even more complex version, which the Germans could not crack.

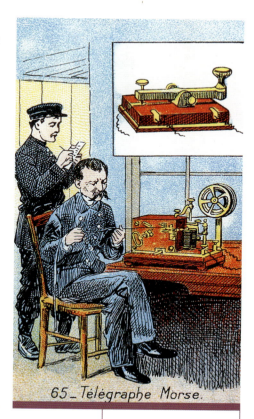

65 _ Télégraphe Morse.

ABOVE This 1910 picture shows a message being received by Morse telegraph, decoded and written down for passing to the intended recipient.

Principles of Codes and Ciphers

Codes and ciphers depend on logical systems that both the sender and the receiver can understand. For example, one of the simplest ciphers just transposes the letters of the plain text. In a transposition cipher, the word "MIDWAY" might have the first pair of letters shuffled to positions 5 and 6, the second pair to positions 1 and 2 and the final pair to positions 3 and 4, producing the group "DWAYMI." If the rest of the message follows suit, these kinds of ciphers can be broken without much difficulty.

Consequently, most ciphers depend on substitution, or sometimes a combination of substitution and transposition. In substitution ciphers, cipher letters replace the normal letters of the alphabet. To confuse outsiders, a series of different cipher alphabets can be used, switching between them according to preset rules — changing for every letter or every 10th letter.

The system used in a particular cipher is the key to that cipher. Often, agents rely on a keyword. British Special Operations Executive agents in Occupied Europe were given poems to use as keys for their messages. Unfortunately, if the Germans could deduce that poem, they could read all of that agent's messages. As a stopgap, SOE agents had poems written just for them. But a captured agent could be forced to reveal the poem, and that meant the Germans could read all their previous messages.

Some espionage networks used book ciphers, where a letter would be identified in a message by its position on a certain page of a particular book, by line, word and individual letter number. Later, SOE agents used "silks," cipher alphabets printed on silk, which would not crackle when hidden within the layers of a garment. Each strip contained a key for the cipher alphabets to be used for a given message. After the message was sent, the strip was torn off and destroyed. Each cipher was only used once, so the system was quite secure. Based on that principle, Russian agents often used "one time pads," creating each message from a different page of a preprinted notebook.

Codes follow the same principles as ciphers, except that whole words are coded rather than individual letters. This means that the sender and the receiver of a coded message must have a complete code dictionary, in order to translate each word into a group of letters or figures. Even so, experts may spot patterns that help them to decode the message.

More recently, systems have been developed that add noise to make the broadcast message sound like atmospheric interference, not worth even recording. But when it reaches the intended station, the covering noise can be stripped away to leave only the message. Currently, scientists are looking for ways to use lasers to scramble and unscramble voice signals sent along fiber-optic communications lines, as a way to protect messages from being intercepted.

Perhaps the strongest system, particularly when using voice messages rather than Morse code, is to employ operators who speak their own language — a language the enemy cannot access or even identify. During World War II, American units spread across the vast Pacific theater kept in touch by using Navajo Indians as radio operators. They spoke to each other in the complex Navajo language, in which a single word can often convey the meaning of a whole sentence.

This language was virtually impossible to learn unless someone began speaking it at birth. Only 28 non-Navajos, who were mostly missionaries and anthropologists, were known to have mastered it, and none of them had any contact with Germany or Japan. Also, a Navajo could spot a non-Navajo, even when that person spoke the language well. Besides, the radio operators came from a tribe of some 50,000 people who usually knew one another already. Any Japanese radio operator who might intercept these messages heard a mixture of Navajo words, American slang and military code words they could not understand.

More recently, British Army units serving with the UN forces in Bosnia used this same principle. They assigned Welsh-speaking soldiers as radio operators to provide secure communications between different elements of a battalion on active service. Welsh is more widely spoken than Navajo and easier to learn, but fluent Welsh speakers were unlikely to exist among the local Serbs, Albanians and Croats.

BELOW A circular code that has been expanded into a table to make enciphering and deciphering easier and more straightforward.

Breaking the Enigma

How was Enigma broken? Despite the awesome number of potential combinations, British experts discovered weaknesses in the system, which reduced the number of possibilities. For example, any letter in the plain message text could be represented by any other letter of the alphabet, with the exception of itself. Second, there was a reciprocal relationship between the plain text letter and its cipher equivalent — if the plain text letter "s" became a "Q" in the cipher text at a particular rotor position and order, and with a given set of plugboard connections, then "q" would be represented by "S" in the cipher text at the same settings.

During this process of trial and error, fast, reliable machines saved months of painstaking work. Code breakers tried certain combinations of letters for messages known to come from a particular source, identified by radio direction finding. Army and Luftwaffe Enigma messages began with six code letters, which helped the recipient figure out which settings had been used. After that, they were usually addressed to a particular unit or individual. Other loopholes included "kisses," slang for two versions of a signal being sent at the same time, one enciphered by Enigma and the other by a lower grade cipher.

To protect this hard-won resource, the Allies hesitated to act on intelligence revealed by Enigma messages unless that same information could have come from another source. For example, relatively early in the war, they read messages detailing the return of German surface raiders

— and Keeping the Secrets

to their home ports in Occupied France. If they had sunk all these warships, the Germans might have guessed their signals were being read. Finally, the Allies decided to attack all but two of them.

Another time, Enigma intercepts revealed the sailing times and routes of Italian supply tankers heading for North Africa. The British sank them so that Rommel's Afrika Korps ran out of fuel and ammunition. To deceive the Germans, the British sent a message in a cipher they knew the enemy could read, thanking a fictitious Italian resistance group for the "tip."

During the Battle of the Atlantic, the Germans began sending supply submarines to keep their U-boats operating for longer periods in distant, target-rich waters. Enigma ciphers gave the positions where the U-boats and the supply submarines were to meet. The Allies read these messages and decided that the benefits of attacking these subs outweighed the risk. During this time, several task groups were at sea, each based around a small escort carrier. If the carrier-borne aircraft searched the area where a supply sub was known to be and attacked it, the encounter could look like a coincidence. Between June and October 1943, the British sank nine of the 10 German tanker subs. Largely because the Allies were able to read Enigma signals, a month later the Germans withdrew from the convoy routes.

OPPOSITE The Colossus electrical digital computer was developed in 1943 to help with cracking the German Enigma signals by running through countless possible combinations to reveal the plain text.

LEFT AND BELOW The four-rotor German Enigma machine was also issued with boxes of alternative rotors having different connections to provide an additional level of security.

DODGING U-BOATS
NORTH ATLANTIC, 1940–43

During the early years of World War II, the German radio interception and cipher breaking service, the B-Dienst, proved extremely clever at reading Royal Navy codes. Their findings helped Hitler successfully to invade Norway in April 1940.

Knowing that the British planned to occupy the strategic port of Narvik in northern Norway, the Germans sent decoy warships toward that region. The British reacted, as the Germans expected, by sending all their naval forces northward. Meanwhile, the Germans landed their occupying army in southern Norway without any Royal Navy opposition. But the B-Dienst's greatest coup was breaking the BAMS — Broadcasting for Allied Merchant Ships — code. On July 10, 1940, the German raiding ship *Atlantis* captured the British merchant ship *City of Baghdad* in the Indian Ocean. When the Germans boarded their prize, they found a set of BAMS code-books and tables. These enabled the radio operator of the *Atlantis* to read messages that guided the raider to other merchant ships.

Finding the Convoys

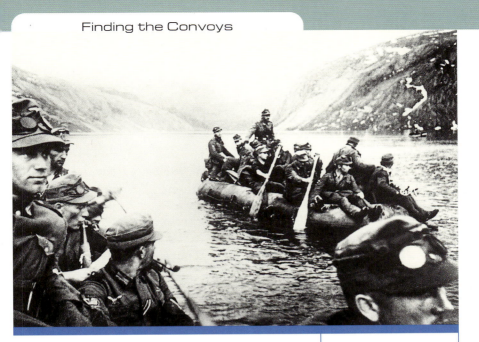

More captured ships gave the Germans still more clues to the British cipher system. By 1941, the B-Dienst were reading messages sent to Allied ships warning them about the positions, timings and routes of the German U-boats. By reading British signals that warned their forces about all known U-boats at sea, the Germans could see what their enemy knew of their whereabouts! While they read each other's signals, Allied convoys were being rerouted to avoid meeting the U-boats. In turn, the U-boats were being rerouted to match the new courses and speeds of the convoys in a grim dance of death.

Later, though, the Allies got their revenge when they broke the German naval Enigma ciphering system. This enabled them to pinpoint the exact locations of the U-boats, from their own signals reporting back to base. Then in May 1943, when the Allies were finally gaining an advantage, the British ciphers were changed. The B-Dienst had to begin the tedious process of breaking the new codes all over again. They failed to succeed in time to save the U-boats.

ABOVE German troops paddle up the Narvik Fjord in inflatable dinghies.

OPPOSITE TOP German field service badge worn by troops who had taken part in the Narvik campaign of 1940.

OPPOSITE BOTTOM British ships bombard German ships.

CRACKING THE PURPLE CIPHERS

US, 1941

The Japanese first used a version of the Enigma machine for communicating with their embassies overseas that American code-breaking experts called "Red." Later, they replaced the machines with a more complex version the Americans called "Purple." The machines used Roman characters, rather than Japanese script, since they were based on the German machine.

ABOVE Basic code-breaking equipment: headphones to intercept radio messages and pads to note down the text for later analysis.

In a brilliant coup, American experts had intercepted prewar radio messages prepared by the Red machines and cracked the ciphers. Eventually, they built their own matching versions of both the Red and Purple machines. Once they broke the Red text, the Americans had a route to decipher Purple messages too. Nevertheless, the US Army's Signal Intelligence Service worked more than 18 months before they deciphered the first full Purple message in August 1940.

One crucial message almost forewarned them that the Japanese would attack Pearl Harbor. This message was picked up by a US Navy station near Seattle, at 1:28 a.m. on December 7, 1941, and deciphered at naval headquarters in Washington, DC. It told the Japanese ambassador to hand a final note to the US government no later than 1 p.m. Washington time that day ending all diplomatic negotiations between the two countries.

At 10:20 a.m., a copy had reached Lieutenant Commander Alwin D. Kramer, a Japanese language expert. He realized that the 1 p.m. deadline implied a surprise attack. One p.m. in Washington would be 7:30 a.m. at the US Pacific Fleet base at Pearl Harbor. But there was nothing in the Japanese message to indicate where an attack might be launched.

Meanwhile, the Japanese carriers were less than 300 miles (500 km) from their target, maintaining strict radio silence. In Washington, the deciphered message reached General Marshall at the War Department. He ordered the signal to be enciphered and radioed to Hawaii and bases on the US Pacific coast, the Philippines and the West Indies.

The signal arrived at the RCA station in Honolulu at 7:33 a.m., December 7. By then, the first wave of Japanese aircraft was showing up on US Army radar, less than 40 miles (60 km) from the island. Meanwhile, the message was placed in a tray to await hand delivery.

Finally, at 7:55 a.m., the first Japanese bomb struck the seaplane ramp in the center of the Pearl Harbor naval base. Clerks at the Japanese embassy in Washington were still struggling to decipher the complex string of messages. As a result, Japan never delivered the declaration of war, which should have preceded the attack. The US believed they had deliberately chosen not to formally declare war and was determined to punish Japan for this treachery.

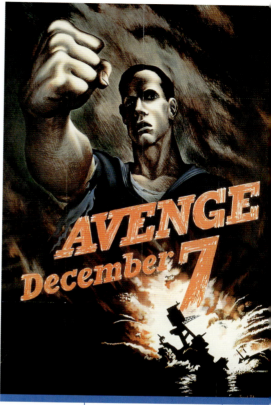

ABOVE The feeling of shock and fury felt by the American people after Pearl Harbor was swiftly followed by a sense of retribution, encapsulated in this **US government poster.**

"ULTRA" AIDS ALLIED FORCES IN THE PACIFIC US, 1942–45

After the United States was catapulted into the war in December 1941, the Americans were able to exploit their brilliant coup in breaking the Japanese ciphers. First, though, they had to break back into the JN25 naval cipher. The Japanese had changed it after American newspapers mentioned the deciphering of messages that revealed the enemy's plans to attack Midway.

Until they cracked JN25, they had to rely on a combination of direction finding and traffic analysis to track the movements of Japanese naval forces. This work was vital during the long fight for the island of Guadalcanal, in the Solomons, and its vital airstrip. By late October 1942, they had partially succeeded, and an "Ultra" (the cover name for the Allies' cipher-breaking efforts, meaning "ultra top secret") bulletin warned the American fleet that the Japanese planned a naval offensive against the island of Guadalcanal.

The greatest coup of the Pacific War began when two Royal New Zealand Navy ships, HMNZS *Kiwi* and HMNZS *Moa*, attacked the Japanese submarine *I-1* off the western tip of Guadalcanal on January 29, 1943. After the *Kiwi* rammed it and forced it aground, crew from the *Moa* retrieved the submarine's cipher tables. These two warships were in place when the *I-1* arrived because deciphered Japanese messages showed that they were sending submarines to aid beleaguered troops on Guadalcanal.

Although the cipher books were outdated when they reached shore, they let American cryptographers read earlier messages that held priceless information about Japanese units, organization and signals procedures. In turn, this information helped them to understand new transmissions. In one message, deciphered on April 14, 1943, they learned that the Japanese naval commander-in-chief, Admiral Yamamoto, America's strongest foe in the Pacific, was planning an airborne tour of bases in the Northern Solomons.

Increasingly, the ability to read Japanese ciphers gave America a vital edge. Advance knowledge of Japanese plans gave the US Navy the upper hand during the rest of the Solomons campaign. Later, US submarines were able to cripple enemy convoys and disrupt their whole resupply and reinforcement system. As they fought throughout the Pacific, American forces could approach islands unseen when they knew the location of Japanese air patrols. When the US prepared to retake the Mariana Islands, swarms of Japanese aircraft attacked the ships of Task Force 58 for eight and a half hours. But the Americans were listening to the radio messages coordinating those strikes, which told them exactly what was coming their way and when. This battle became known as "The Great Marianas Turkey Shoot," and the huge losses of trained air crew all but crippled the Japanese naval air arm.

In other Pacific battles, American cryptanalysts were able to help defeat the Imperial Japanese Navy at the "Battle of Leyte Gulf," when they took back the Philippines. These experts made it possible to hunt down individual warships that were frantically trying to escape Allied aircraft. Even the last desperate throw of the kamikaze suicide strikes on the US fleet attacking the islands of Iwo Jima and Okinawa was signaled over radio channels monitored by the Americans. Intercepting these signals gave enough warning to reduce their terrible effect.

ABOVE The end of Japanese air power, as another aircraft crashes into the sea during the "Great Marianas Turkey Shoot" of June 1944.

OPPOSITE A Japanese cruiser is left burning and helpless at the "Battle of Leyte Gulf" in October 1944, when Japanese intentions and movements were revealed by reading their signals.

"CIPHER WARS": PROTECTING THE "ULTRA" SECRETS
UK, 1940–45

Both the British and Americans dreaded the possibility that they might show their hand by acting upon information they gained from reading their enemies' ciphers. If their opponents switched to a totally new system, the resulting intelligence blackout would be catastrophic. Yet failing to act on vital information could mean losing a battle or a campaign. Thus the whole cipher war became a delicate balancing act.

ABOVE Admiral Isoruku Yamamoto, Commander in Chief of the Imperial Japanese Navy, shot down and killed by American fighters in a triumph of cipher analysis.

OPPOSITE TOP Karl Doenitz, a submarine officer in World War I, was commander of the U-boats, and later of the whole German Navy, in World War II.

For safety reasons, this information was given only to senior commanders, and the actual source of the information was hidden under the cover name "Ultra." Even then, it was difficult to conceal things. American General Douglas MacArthur was so pleased when Admiral Yamamoto was shot down that he wanted to publicize the success. But the Joint Chiefs of Staff ordered that it be kept secret until the Japanese announced the admiral's death.

In the "Battle of the Atlantic," it was difficult to hide the results of reading German signals between the U-boat commander, Admiral Doenitz, and the submarines operating at sea. The Allies could order ships to change their courses and avoid the threat, so the Germans could not be sure they were acting on precise information and did not immediately think their machine ciphers had been cracked. As in World War I, they assumed that their Enigma systems and their safeguards, were so strong that the Allies could not read their signals.

The Germans did not hear the alarm bells even when messages from German prisoners-of-war, using

Protecting "Ultra"

prearranged codes in letters sent back home, revealed that Allied sailors had boarded their ships. They were convinced that regular changes in machine settings, and the huge number of possible relationships between each letter of the message and its ciphered equivalent, made Enigma foolproof. Besides, they had no idea how many brilliant mathematicians and cryptanalysts were working with number-crunching machines to crack the code.

BELOW Lockheed P38 Lightning long-range fighters had the endurance to reach and shoot down Admiral Yamamoto's plane on information derived from secret Japanese ciphers.

3

ELECTRONIC SECRETS — ON THE GROUND

Ideally, espionage and intelligence information would flow only inward, with no useful material reaching the other side. But in reality, information flows in every possible direction. And while some of it may be valuable, the opposition can also plant false information in order to mislead its enemies. The world of secret agents becomes even more complex with the presence of multiple agents and human loyalties that can change from one side to the other.

That same two-way flow of information affects the world of electronic and communications intelligence. Systems that are designed to provide information, say on the location of targets or the approach of hostile aircraft, tend to betray themselves as soon as they begin to operate. Important radio messages can be revealing. Even if no messages are deciphered, an electronic eavesdropper can find out a lot from the

RIGHT AND OPPOSITE BELOW Power projection: the American nuclear aircraft carrier USS *George Washington* in the Northern Gulf, as flight-deck crews prepare aircraft for some of the 80–100 sorties flown each day over the "no–fly" zones of Iraq.

level of traffic, the length of the messages and the locations of the transmitters.

In the world of electronic intelligence, traffic analysis can help to build a detailed picture of an adversary's defenses, bases, weaponry, movements and capabilities. An operator can also use the information revealed through electronic intelligence to make it false, incomplete or misleading. By studying all aspects of the intelligence picture, agents can spot gaps or inconsistencies.

Conflicts on the High Seas

During the later Cold War years, the Soviet Union was keen to develop a strong deep-water navy, equal to that of the US Navy. Yet, the Americans had one huge advantage: the carrier battle groups. Each group was centered on a nuclear-powered aircraft carrier that could circle the globe without needing to refuel. It could launch a devastating air strike anywhere in the world, with nuclear or conventional weapons, often beyond the range of any kind of land-based air power.

The Americans and British had developed the basic technology and tactics, so carrier warfare evolved from a body of knowledge that the Soviets lacked. They faced the task of having to design carriers and the appropriate

aircraft from scratch. This meant studying the basics of carrier operation as closely as possible. At the time, the US Navy was running the only game in town, as its carrier groups held joint exercises with the navies of their NATO allies.

As a result, Soviet aircraft, warships and even fishing trawlers — loaded with electronics as well as fishing gear — showed up to observe every US exercise. Eager for information, they recorded radio transmissions, frequencies and the locations of transmitters in the traffic between ships and aircraft, which told much about how the carriers operated. The electronic signatures of radar systems, including the power, frequency, pulse rate and other data, could make them easier to identify and easier to jam or mislead if a real conflict occurred.

ABOVE Photographs of a Soviet spy trawler, taken by a Royal Air Force aircraft on a reconnaissance flight over the Atlantic, are examined by an RAF intelligence officer.

At times, these surface ships edged dangerously close to opposing warships. There were often near misses, even collisions as a result of errors, wrong decisions and misjudging another captain's intentions.

Spotting Submarines

Besides these risky surface clashes, the submarine version was being fought deep in the oceans. This information was even more vital to national survival, because the major powers relied on ballistic-missile submarines to deliver the mighty blows that deterred each nation from using nuclear weapons. Knowing the routes these submarines would follow to their wartime stations would provide a valuable early warning if a conflict began to erupt.

Once, sound waves were used to locate submerged submarines, but they can also reveal the searching sub's position while looking for its target. All the hunter-killer submarines can do is listen for the sound signatures of enemy craft in the otherwise silent depths. Often, only the tiniest variations in the beat of the propeller, or the shape of the waveforms of the sound signal, can show whether the submarine belongs to friend or foe. Based on such clues, a captain may have to decide whether to launch a nuclear torpedo or take evasive action.

As each side produced new designs, or changed existing models to make them run more quietly, and thus harder to detect, every navy had to push closer to one another's submarines to record and identify the noises they made. The Americans had installed a monitoring system called SOSUS (Sound Surveillance System) on the seabed of a part of the GIUK (Greenland-Iceland-UK) Gap, through which most Russian subs passed en route to the open Atlantic. SOSUS could pick up undersea noises over a vast area, which made it even more crucial to be able to identify the noises made by every class of active Russian warship. Here, too, accidents happened. There were collisions between massive underwater craft maneuvering too close for comfort, or simply disasters that occurred as people operated every day in the dangerous undersea environment.

ABOVE The crew onboard the US Navy nuclear submarine *USS Bosie* keeps lookout as it moves along the ocean surface.

Double, Triple and Multiple Agents

Because double agents often are highly placed in their own country's defense, government or intelligence organization, they can offer valuable information. But an apparent double agent may be a deliberate plant from the opposition and the information they deliver may be laced with deception. Even when a double agent is genuine, fear or greed, or lingering loyalty to their own country, can lead them to switch sides again, to become a treble or even multiple agent.

One of the most complex agents in espionage history was Ignatz, or Isaac Trebitsch, born into a Hungarian Jewish family in 1879. After giving up rabbinical studies, he moved to London at age 17 and joined the Church of England. Then he went to Germany and on to Canada, where he was ordained as an Anglican minister. At age 30, he returned to London, changed his surname to Lincoln and became a British citizen. After serving briefly in Parliament, he became a journalist. In 1912, he reported on the Balkan Wars and became a double agent for Bulgaria and Turkey. He was arrested for his activities but the Germans had him released so quickly from a Bulgarian jail that it seemed certain he had been working for Berlin.

Trebitsch returned to London and tried to join British Intelligence. When they rejected him, he moved to the US, but was extradited to the UK for fraud, and jailed, before being deported to his native Hungary in 1919. From there, he returned to Germany, where he took part in an unsuccessful revolt against the government in 1920. Now it was on to China, where Chinese Nationalists hired him as an agent against the independent warlords, though he was rumored to be a double agent for the Japanese. He converted to Buddhism, and became an abbot with the Chinese name Chao Kung. He died there in 1943.

Not all double agents have such a complex and nomadic life. William Sebold was a German-born American. While visiting his mother in Germany in 1939, he was blackmailed by the Gestapo and forced into joining the Abwehr. He alerted American authorities, who arranged for him to work in the US as a double agent. He informed them about German spy networks in America and sent false information back to his controllers. Later, Sebold testified as a witness in the trials of German spies captured in America.

The Spanish-born Juan Garcia was probably the most successful double agent of all time. During World War II, he volunteered to work for British Intelligence but was turned down. Then he contacted the German Abwehr and was hired as an agent and sent to the UK, where he contacted the British. This time he was hired, as a double agent. Under his codename "Garbo," he played a vital role in feeding the Germans misinformation in the Fortitude D-Day deceptions campaign. As a result, the Germans decided to keep massive forces tied up waiting for an attack in the wrong location, while the Normandy beachhead was firmly established

TOP AND ABOVE Juan Pujol Garcia volunteered to serve as an Allied double agent, and subsequently was recruited by the Germans under their codename "Cato." Known to the Allies as "Garbo," he fed the Abwehr carefully prepared Allied misinformation, which played a vital part in the D-Day deceptions.

The Relentless Search for Clues

Similar confrontations have occurred high in the stratosphere. During the Cold War years, Russian patrol aircraft would approach British airspace by skirting to the north of Norway. Although Royal Air Force fighters would escort these Soviet aircraft out of UK territory, the process itself gave the Russians valuable information. For example, the Soviet fliers would know when they were picked up by British early-warning radar, giving them range, frequency and location of the ground stations involved. Their own radar would show where the fighters came from, and they could determine their climb performance by seeing how long it took before they appeared alongside. The length of time they stayed in formation before being relieved showed their operating endurance.

During the height of the Cold War, both sides continually sought information. For years, the West recorded and analyzed signals traffic of Warsaw Pact units. The number of messages showed them the level of traffic, and cross-bearings from direction finders showed the location of each transmitter. Over time, specific combinations of callsigns and frequencies could be linked to tank or infantry units, or brigade or divisional headquarters. A sharp increase in traffic meant an increase in the state of readiness or the running of a major military exercise. If many units moved closer to the border, this suggested that opposing forces were going on full alert.

Since the Warsaw Pact broke up, East and West have built a new relationship and the pattern of electronic intelligence-gathering has changed dramatically. However, the search for information from potential enemies is still thriving — only those enemies have changed. Knowledge is power, especially in the complex and competitive world of military electronic intelligence.

TUNNEL VISION
US, UK, AUSTRIA AND GERMANY, 1949–56

Not all espionage successes involve agents penetrating enemy territory to collect data and bring it back to their controllers. In 1953 when the US commissioned a new embassy in Moscow, the KGB moved in with the builders. They hid more than 40 microphones in the structure to relay top-secret conversations to Soviet ears. Much damage was done before the bugs were discovered.

ABOVE A Russian soldier examines the inside of the tunnel to check for telephone-tapping equipment.

Likewise, Western intelligence services managed to eavesdrop on their Cold War enemies by tunneling into their communications systems. The first such coup occurred in 1951, when Austria — like Germany — was still occupied by the four Allied powers: Russia, the US, Britain and France. Each nation directed a different zone of the country, and the capital, Vienna, was split among them. The four Allied headquarters were close to one another in the center of this compact city. Furthermore, all the telephone networks for Austria were routed through Vienna, in a complex web that crisscrossed throughout the various zones.

The British Secret Intelligence Service proceeded to dig a tunnel beneath their headquarters. Code-named Operation Silver, the tunnel let them tap into the telephone lines that ran to Soviet headquarters. Since the most important messages were in code, they needed to decipher it, and their American colleagues in the CIA found the key. Ironically, a defect in one of the CIA's own cipher machines helped them crack the Russian codes. Tests had shown that when the operator typed the clear text into the machine, the process sent a faint signal revealing the plain text. The CIA machine was scrapped. But knowing about the problem led them to wonder: Did the Russian machines have the same flaw? They did, and for several years, the delighted intelligence operators gathered sensitive information that proved invaluable in Cold War power-politics.

Later came the more spectacular Operation Gold, in Occupied Berlin. Using information supplied by the German spymaster Reinhard Gehlen, once again the SIS and the CIA dug a tunnel from Western territory. It ran for 500 yards (450 m), at a depth of 15 feet (4.5 m), to tap into the Russian landlines running from their Berlin headquarters to Leipzig in the east, then on to other destinations in eastern Europe and the Soviet Union.

This tunnel should have been doomed, since a Russian double agent knew about the plans. But the Russians let the operation continue, rather than risk revealing that they had a "mole" spying on the Western side. They were not aware of any weakness in their cipher machines and thought their codes were unbreakable.

After US Army engineers finished the tunnel early in 1955, the CIA began taping. Each line carried multiple conversations at the same time. The equipment installed at the head of the tunnel was recording up to 1,200 hours of material daily on 600 tape recorders, producing 800 tapes a day. These were flown to London and Washington.

Operation Gold continued for 14 months. In the spring of 1956, heavy rain caused water to seep into telephone cables in East Berlin. When the East German engineers dug up the cables to make repairs, they discovered the tunnel, which their Russian masters had kept a secret. The information channel was cut off, but not before the Western allies had gained key political and military information.

ABOVE The Russian double agent George Blake betrayed the SIS/CIA tunnel in Berlin to his Soviet spymasters, but eventually was caught and sentenced to 42 years in prison.

STALKING SUBMARINES

US AND RUSSIA, 1969

One of the most successful American spy submarines during the late 1960s was the hunter-killer USS *Lapon*. She excelled at the risky task of snooping on the growing Soviet nuclear sub force. Her successes began in March 1969. While patrolling through the icy Barents Sea, she made the first clear sighting of the Soviet version of the American *Polaris* missile submarines, the Yankee-class nuclear ballistic missile sub. The commander took a series of photographs through the periscope to give the West its best views yet of this powerful new threat.

Knowing what the Yankees looked like was useful, but the US needed information on their performance, maneuverability and audio signatures, so that anyone passing in sonar range of one would recognize the sounds they heard. The only sure way to find out was to tail one of the Yankees for as long as possible, without the Russian crew noticing the Americans' presence.

Trailing a Yankee would be difficult and risky. When the *Lapon* received the call on September 16, she was ready. She reached her target destination, off the Denmark Strait between Iceland and Greenland, a day before the Russian showed up. There followed nearly four days of hide-and-seek, during which the Yankee's sounds were often drowned out by the clamor of marine life and nearby fishing boats. After that, the Soviet boat turned on a steady course, allowing the *Lapon* to follow close behind. Then, after 18 hours, she made an unpredicted turn and disappeared. No sound trace remained, and the audio scent was lost.

ABOVE The launching of the US Navy hunter-killer nuclear submarine USS *Lapon*.

After several frustrating days, the *Lapon's* sonar team heard the faint sounds of the approaching Yankee. This time, Commander Mack was determined not to lose the Russian, and he closed to within half a mile of his quarry. For the rest of the voyage, the *Lapon* hung on grimly, trying to match every twist and turn of the Soviet vessel, while the crew recorded the noises she made. They avoided making any unnecessary sounds themselves, since even a slammed compartment door or the dropping of a wrench would have tipped off the Russians.

BELOW Nuclear submarines can dive suddenly and almost without trace to seek the protection of the depths, where pursuit is more difficult.

For the next 47 days, the crew mapped out the Yankee's operational area and tracked her through regular sharp turns, including several that traced a complete circle. Despite some close calls, the American sub managed to remain undetected. Finally, the Yankee finished her patrol and turned straight toward her own coastal waters. Duty done, the *Lapon* was able to go home too.

OPERATION RYAN
SOVIET UNION, 1980

By 1980, relations between the two superpowers were becoming chilly. After the Soviets invaded Afghanistan late in 1979, the US responded by refusing to ratify the second Strategic Arms Limitation Treaty (SALT II) and then boycotted the 1980 Olympic Games. They elected a president, Ronald Reagan, whom the Soviets thought would approach foreign relations as a hawk, not a dove.

ABOVE Ronald Reagan takes the oath of office as the 40th President of the US, administered by Chief Justice Warren Burger. Reagan's wife Nancy looks on.

By 1981, Soviet leaders feared the US and NATO were preparing for war and ordered the KGB to learn as much as possible. As part of an operation code-named RYAN, they used all their communications surveillance technology and ground stations in Russia, eastern Europe and especially in Cuba, which was ideally placed to overhear messages between the US and her European allies and US forces overseas.

Other, more unexpected, listening posts were located right in US territory. Three buildings in Washington, DC, were festooned with communications gear. These were the old and new Soviet embassies, and a building that served as the headquarters for the Soviet military attaché. There were four sites in New York City — one located within the Soviet mission to the United Nations, another at the Soviet diplomatic residential complex in Riverdale and two at Soviet diplomatic recreational facilities on Long Island. Other listening posts were maintained in Maryland, and at Soviet consular offices in Chicago and San Francisco.

All of these monitoring stations could overhear phone conversations between official limousines and government offices at the State Department, the Pentagon and CIA headquarters. The Maryland post could also gather signals to and from the Atlantic Fleet headquarters at Norfolk, Virginia, and at Langley Air Force Base. In Europe, similar eavesdropping was conducted from diplomatic sites in the UK, Western Germany, France, the Netherlands, Norway and Italy.

What were the Soviets looking for? They believed certain events indicated more readiness for war.

These included the rising propaganda efforts against the Soviet bloc, the sending of sabotage teams to Warsaw Pact territory and a crackdown against Communist sympathizers in the West. Intelligence organizations tend to see what they expect to see, as several events soon showed. On March 23, 1983, President Reagan made his famous "evil empire" speech, denouncing the Soviet Union's tyranny and hostile actions. He also made the first reference to the "Star Wars" anti-ballistic-missile defense system. On June 9, Reagan's staunchest ally, Margaret Thatcher, was re-elected as British prime minister, which added to Soviet paranoia. The stage was set for an event to trigger an explosive reaction.

ABOVE An aerial view of the Pentagon, for 50 years the military nerve center of the US and the world's largest office building.

BELOW The special relationship between the USA and UK during the 1980s was founded on the rapport between President Reagan and Margaret Thatcher, seen here during the President's visit to England in 1982.

4

FAKES AND FRAUDS: DELIBERATE DECEPTIONS

In addition to stunning successes, the history of espionage is riddled with failures that can result from too little training, human error and pure bad luck. Disaster can strike when an agent is caught, especially if their agency does not know. The captors may turn the seized agent into one of their own or use them to send planted messages. For that reason, intelligence services craft their planted messages very carefully to avoid suspicion and to hide their actions, plans or capabilities.

Imagine, for instance, that a KGB agent has been captured by, or has defected to, the West. The agent's messages continue, so at first the KGB has no real cause for alarm. But in order to serve the West's purpose without revealing too much, the planted information will need some basis in truth. The KGB will compare it with earlier messages and notice any sudden change in the intelligence picture. If a message contains facts they can check on their own, the KGB probably will do so. The double agent's controllers may even include sensitive material that the KGB would not expect to receive in a misleading report. However, the possible benefit must make up for losing that information.

Like other aspects of espionage, the use of false information has a long tradition. The Chinese military master, Sun Tzu, offered these principles 25 centuries ago: A commander should "when capable, feign incapacity, when active, inactivity ... when near, make it appear that you are far away; when far away, that you are near." He advised the leader to "offer the enemy a bait to lure him; feign disorder and strike him."

A Duke Steals a March on His Rivals

Since that era, great commanders have raised the art of military deceptions. One expert was John Churchill, Duke of Marlborough, who fought with the Dutch and Germans against the French and Bavarians. In 1704, Marlborough led his army to the Rhine, while his French opponents, under Marshal Tallard, awaited his next blow. At Coblenz, Marlborough's army crossed the Rhine on a bridge of boats, then marched on upriver.

Tallard's network of spies went to work. His agent reported that British engineers were building another bridge of boats about 120 miles (190 km) farther up the river. This would allow Marlborough's army to cross back to the western bank. Concluding that the British would attack Alsace, Tallard ordered his troops to march south, where they could prepare a surprise attack on the British.

To Tallard's dismay, the bridge-building was a deliberate piece of misinformation. While the French marched south, Marlborough moved east to join his German allies on the Danube, 500 miles (800 km) from where the French were waiting. When Tallard finally realized that he had been misled, he set off in pursuit, driving his troops in a series of forced marches. The British and Germans awaited him near a Danube village named Blenheim and Tallard's exhausted troops were easily defeated. This was surely one of Marlborough's greatest victories, leading to the destruction of the French Army, the capture of Marshal Tallard and the collapse of their Bavarian allies.

ABOVE The "Battle of Blenheim," where Marlborough and his German allies defeated the French on August 13, 1704.

OPPOSITE Monsier le Maréchal de Tallard, Marlborough's vanquished and outsmarted adversary.

ABOVE George Washington was able to make good use of undercover agents and secret intelligence in the campaigns of the Revolutionary War.

BELOW RIGHT Dummy horses designed to convince the Turks that the British attack would be delivered against their Gaza positions.

Other commanders have successfully baffled their opponents by laying a trail of false intelligence. During the American War of Independence, George Washington left papers for his British enemies to capture, suggesting that his strength was much greater than it really was. To conceal his casualties, they were buried at night, in unmarked graves.

Disinformation is also valuable in peacetime espionage, but in wartime the stakes are usually higher. During both world wars, the simplest of materials, combined with great ingenuity, often produced fantastic results. Very often, as was true in Marlborough's campaign against the French, planners try to deceive an opponent as to where they will strike next. Although methods of disguising and sending information may change, the purpose and value of the coup remain the same.

Deceiving the Turks

During World War I, the British General Allenby led a tough campaign against the Turks in Palestine. To defeat a strong Turkish defensive position at Gaza, Allenby decided to outflank them by moving his forces east and attacking Beersheba. This scheme was doomed if the enemy suspected his plans. Since the Turks might spot any troop movements toward Beersheba, the British had to convince them that their actual target was Gaza.

Of course, the Turks were far more likely to believe this deception if they found out the details for themselves. One of Allenby's officers, Colonel Richard Meinertzhagen, headed for the "no man's land" in front of the Turkish positions. When a Turkish patrol started firing, he hastily fled, dropping a water bottle, a pack and a pair of binoculars. The pack had been prepared very carefully in advance. It was partly soaked in horse's blood to imply that Meinertzhagen had been shot by Turkish bullets, and then dropped it in his weakened condition.

The sack held some papers, money, a cipher book and a letter from the officer's wife. Some of the papers referred to a planned attack on Beersheba and mentioned the original date for the attack, which the Turks' own spies might well have uncovered. The papers also showed those plans had been changed: Gaza was the new target, but the British were planning moves to convince the Turks that Beersheba would be hit.

ABOVE The outcome of the successful deception: After driving the Turks out of Jerusalem, British troops guard the Jaffa Gate.

This plan had enough basis in truth to fit with other information Turkish intelligence had collected. Later, the British radioed messages using the cipher that the Turks had captured, claiming that Meinertzhagen had been court-martialed for losing the pack. They secretly moved their cavalry toward Beersheba, leaving dummy horses made of straw in their original positions. Heavy radio traffic in the Gaza area, and relative silence around Beersheba, strengthened the deception.

This clever disinformation plot achieved priceless results. The Turks were astounded by the attack at Beersheba, which began with a shattering bombardment from hidden artillery, followed by a cavalry charge. The defenders set off in full retreat, and the panic spread to Gaza, where a follow-up attack took these Turkish defenses too. Within six weeks, Allenby's army had captured Jerusalem.

Confusing Impressions

Similar ploys were carried out in World War II. During their victorious campaign in France, the Germans used several "black" radio stations, which pretended to be French transmitters giving the people vital information. They emphasized how far and how fast German troops were advancing, and urged people to cash in their savings, causing a run on the banks and floods of refugees to jam the roads.

In addition, German agents wearing French uniforms parachuted behind the lines to give false and conflicting orders that stalled French defenses. This caused people to question essential orders from genuine French soldiers and civilian officials, creating even more confusion. Later, the Germans tried this same tactic in Britain, by dropping hundreds of empty parachutes, each hinting at a spy

BELOW A patrol of the British Home Guard, the citizens' volunteer militia raised to guard against a German invasion of Britain in 1940, arrests suspected enemy agents during an exercise.

OPPOSITE A member of the Home Guard demonstrates the use of camouflage designed to give the advantage of surprise if the enemy should appear.

or German supporter. In response, Britain formed the Home Guard, whose primary job was to deal with this non-existent force.

A Map Trap in North Africa

In the crucial North African campaign of World War II, the German Afrika Korps had pushed the British Eighth Army most of the way back toward Cairo and the Suez Canal by the late summer of 1942. The British, who occupied a restricted 40-mile (65 km) gap near the northern coast, knew they had to stop Rommel by persuading him to attack their strongest defensive position, the ridge at Alam Halfa. It was protected in front by a tract of soft sand that would cause tanks to bog down, while a line of hidden anti-tank guns lay behind. The British devised a cunning plan of misinformation.

Knowing that the Germans had few good, accurate desert maps of their own, the army's intelligence experts created false documents for the enemy. These maps showed that the sand was soft and treacherous to the north-east, where the Germans might otherwise have aimed the attack for Cairo. On the other hand, they indicated that there was good hard sand, capable of supporting armored vehicles, leading up to the Alam Halfa ridge. If the Germans accepted these maps, they would surely fall into the trap.

Now the British had to plant these documents. One map was carried by a patrol of two armored cars that ventured into "no man's land" between the British and German positions. Predictably, the Germans began firing at them. In a carefully rehearsed scenario, one car "broke down" with shells exploding all around. The crew abandoned their vehicle and the second armored car carried them to safety. In the abandoned car, the Germans found a battered map, covered in sand and stained with oil. A second copy was left in the wreckage of a jeep that had been blown up by a German mine in another part of "no man's land." A third and final copy was

ABOVE Dummy tanks being assembled in a British workshop.

BELOW General Bernard L. Montgomery, the new commander of the British Eighth Army in North Africa, and victor of the "Battle of Alamein" over his German adversary, Rommel.

among documents in an officer's briefcase. This was left on a seat in a Cairo bar patronized by German agents. When military police entered the bar to retrieve the case, they found that it was empty. The British spread rumors that a certain Major Smith had been court-martialed for negligence in losing confidential papers and even that he had been executed by firing squad.

What would the Germans do with this misinformation? Early in September 1942, they attacked — and it became clear that they were using the false maps. The Afrika Korps moved through concealed minefields and into the soft sand in front of the Alam Halfa ridge, where concealed British tanks and anti-tank guns fired at their stranded tanks. After three days of mounting losses, they were forced to withdraw. It was Rommel's last attempt to reach Cairo. Now it was clear to both sides that the British would soon attack at Alamein. For the German defenders, the only questions would be: Where? And when?

Deception at Alamein

Rommel knew that General Montgomery's Eighth Army could either attack the northern end of the German front or the southern. With a limited number of tanks available to him, and with chronic fuel shortages, Rommel had to predict his opponents' next move. Despite the growing Allied air superiority, German reconnaissance patrols tried to spot telltale signs of attack preparations.

The flat, featureless desert made concealment nearly impossible and everything the German airmen saw added up to one clear message — the attack would come at the southern end. First of all, the largest supply dumps were being assembled in the south, with masses of tanks and guns. This was confirmed by high levels of Allied radio traffic sent by units in the southern sector. Most reassuring of all, the British seemed to be building a water pipeline across the desert. By measuring its rate of progress, the Germans knew that the British could not attack until November.

Unfortunately, this picture was utterly false. The tanks and guns in the south were dummies, made from wood and canvas and by disguising trucks. Most of the British armaments were really in the north, disguised as trucks and old supply dumps. Radio transmissions between units in the south were mostly false, while genuine units in the north maintained radio silence as far as possible. Even the water pipeline was a dummy, built from flattened water cans, but looking genuine to airmen who were flying overhead.

As a result, when Montgomery's troops attacked the northern end of the front on October 23, 1942, Rommel's armored troops were in the wrong place. Rommel himself was in a German hospital, so the Afrika Korps had to fight this crucial battle without his inspired and quick-thinking leadership. After days of bitter fighting, the Germans began to pull out. Their retreat from Alamein would take them along the length of the North African coast to distant Tunisia where they surrendered seven months later.

ABOVE A dummy pumphouse and reservoir were part of the water pipeline project, being designed to look completely convincing from the air.

BELOW Dummy soldiers manning a trench position to mislead the enemy as to the whereabouts of the main mass of British infantry.

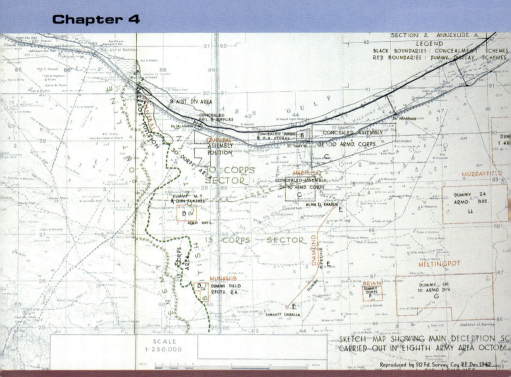

The Alamein deception, and the even more ambitious Fortitude deceptions, which protected the Normandy landings in 1944, laid the basis for later misinformation campaigns. Compared with the deceptions of individual commanders in previous eras, today's false leads must present a much more complex and multifaceted picture. Many different channels of information — spies, radio traffic, reconnaissance flights, satellites and newspaper reports — must all tell the same, ultimately convincing, story.

ABOVE Papers from the headquarters of the Middle East Forces show details of the main deception schemes devised for the Alamein campaign in the fall of 1942.

BELOW A tank is camouflaged as a supply truck to help conceal Allied strength and intentions.

Fortitude – the D-Day Deceptions

RIGHT Maintaining the Fortitude deceptions prior to D-Day meant providing huge numbers of dummy forces in south-eastern England to attract the attention of the German reconnaissance flights: a dummy Spitfire fighter **(TOP)**, a sketchy framework for a dummy hurricane fighter-bomber **(CENTER)** and a framework that could be fitted to a Jeep to make it look like a Sherman tank from the air **(BOTTOM)**.

Fortitude — the D-Day Deceptions cont.

In their ambitious Fortitude campaign, the British and Americans succeeded in keeping a whole German army out of the Normandy fighting until it was too late. This shrewdly organized plan used double agents, electronic intelligence, radar intelligence, communications intelligence and false intelligence.

Once the Allies had decided to land at Normandy, they staged a massive campaign to convince the Germans they would land in the Pas de Calais. First, all the German agents working for Britain sent a series of carefully coordinated messages that said massive forces were being assembled in the south-east of England. Meanwhile, no signs revealed the real troop build-up in the south-west.

All other channels of information reinforced this picture: false radio signals were sent from transmitters in the south-east. Dummy tanks, guns, aircraft and landing craft were massed in fields and river estuaries in the east to fool German reconnaissance aircraft. When Allied aircraft began pre-invasion attacks on German forces in France, they attacked three targets in Pas de Calais for every two in Normandy.

At the heart of the hoax was the wholly fictitious FUSAG (First US Army Group), earmarked for the Calais landings, commanded by General George S. Patton. Calculated leaks revealed that he was in eastern England, and the German spies, directed by their Allied spymasters, sent back information describing false troop movements.

When the landing forces actually sailed, a new deception campaign swung into action. Allied bombers destroyed the German radar stations watching the entire Channel coast, except for two in the Pas de Calais area. To dupe them, Royal Air Force bomber squadrons spent the night flying an exact pattern that allowed them to drop metallic foil strips. These created echoes on German radar imitating a huge invasion force approaching across the Channel at low speed. In case the Germans sent naval craft to investigate, the Allied navy had launched a small fleet of motorboats, each towing a large radar-reflecting balloon. Sound equipment on board reproduced the noise of engines and loudspeaker commands.

On land, dummy parachutists were dropped all over the invasion area, loaded with firecrackers to simulate small-arms fire. Small Special Forces teams were also dropped with record players and loudspeakers. These created the sounds of pitched battle in the darkness, confusing the German defenders as to the enemy's positions.

Once the landings began, the Germans obviously would see the truth and act accordingly. But the Allies found brilliant ways to confuse them even more. Their agents in Britain reminded the German spymasters that huge forces still remained in south-eastern England. Vital information from their most respected agent of all, Garbo, fueled these fears. Allied controllers had Garbo tell the Germans that two British units were heading for Normandy, on the grounds that the Germans would soon discover the units' presence for themselves. This information maintained Garbo's credibility.

At that moment, the Germans were about to order seven divisions to move from the Pas de Calais to crush the Normandy invasion. But Garbo sent another message which explained that Normandy was just a feint attack, intended to lure the powerful German Fifteenth Army from Pas de Calais. Once the Germans took the bait and moved their troops westward, the real Allied blow would fall behind them, and with it Pas de Calais. The Germans were sure that by holding back their strongest units, they could foil the Allied plan, so they kept the Fifteenth Army in place for six weeks. By the time they realized that FUSAG was a hoax, Patton was in Normandy, leading forces that eventually would sweep through northern France and drive the Germans back to their own borders.

OPPOSITE LEFT General George S. Patton, commander of the entirely fictitious First US Army Group in the D-Day deceptions, and later the architect of the Allied armored breakout from the Normandy beachhead.

OPERATION MINCEMEAT
ENGLAND AND SPAIN, 1943

After the Germans surrendered in North Africa, the Allies resolved to keep them from guessing they planned to invade southern Sicily to provide a base for later landings on the Italian mainland. Instead, they hoped to convince them their target was Greece.

ABOVE Some of the carefully selected evidence carried on the body to establish "Major Martin's" identity.

How could they achieve this deception? A careless radio message would not work, since the Germans knew only too well that the most important messages were carried in locked briefcases, chained to a courier's wrist. So how could a courier fall convincingly into enemy hands, with the vital information still intact?

The Allies decided their best bet was to let the Germans know that an aircraft carrying a courier and his secret documents had crashed into the sea. A case containing "sensitive documents" could wash up on the Spanish coast. One snag remained, however — the courier's body would have to be washed ashore still chained to the case.

This ruse, called Operation Mincement, required a recently dead body, in a condition that would suggest death by drowning. A London coroner produced the corpse of a young man who had died from pneumonia. The body was clothed in Royal Marines uniform and given documents that identified him as Major William Martin. His briefcase contained letters from the office of the Chief of the Imperial General Staff and from Lord Louis Mountbatten to officers of General Alexander, commanding in the Mediterranean.

The letters were carefully written. Rather than announcing that the Allies were planning to land in

Greece, they discussed detail changes in the plan, which the recipients would already know about, but which would be news to the Germans. They described deceptive actions that the Allies were taking to convince the Germans and Italians that the landings would occur on Sicily instead. One letter claimed that the Allies were staging practice landings on the Tunisian coast and heavy attacks on Sicilian airfields.

The body of "Major Martin" and the vital briefcase were loaded onto a Royal Navy submarine, which surfaced off the Spanish coast on the night of April 30, 1943. Then the corpse was lowered into the water at a spot where the currents would carry it ashore near the port of Huelva, where German diplomats were active.

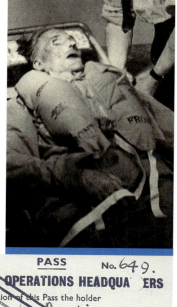

The British insisted on the return of the body, and the case and its contents. Two weeks later, the Spanish authorities handed them over. All the documents were still in their sealed envelopes but laboratory tests showed that they had been opened and resealed.

Ten weeks after the body washed up on a Spanish beach, only two German divisions were defending the Sicilian coast. Powerful German armored divisions had been switched to Greece and Crete, along with naval units that might have disrupted the landing forces. Although the campaign to liberate Sicily was hard-fought, it ended with the Germans having to flee to mainland Italy.

After the war, captured documents showed that German Military Intelligence had doubted the documents were authentic, but Adolf Hitler had been sure that they were genuine. The Operation Mincemeat deception was totally successful.

TOP The body of "Major William Martin" of the Royal marines, dressed in uniform with a life preserver and showing all the postmortem signs associated with drowning after an airplane crash.

ABOVE "Major Martin's" pass, admitting him to Combined Operations Headquarters, showed the documents he carried were important so they would appear genuine.

BOGUS RADIO BROADCASTS

ENGLAND, 1941–45

Perhaps the ultimate false information is a completely fake broadcasting service. During World War II, both sides used this tactic, called "black" radio. "Black" propaganda recognizes that people will pay more attention to material that comes from "their side." This carefully crafted material — written, spoken or visual — must be entirely convincing and it must have a background of truth.

ABOVE William Joyce in "disguise" as Hitler.

The Germans set up their "black" station as the "New British Broadcasting Service." The station pretended to be on the side of the British people, but against their government — and definitely anti-German. This was in sharp contrast to the anti-allied propaganda of official "white" German radio, delivered by a team led by William Joyce, who was nicknamed "Lord Haw Haw" because he spoke with a drawl. But British listeners found this station oddly unconvincing and they paid it little attention.

The British, however, became masters of "black" broadcasting. Their first station was called Gustav Siegfried Eins, from German signallers' jargon for GS1, which could seem to stand for Secret Transmitter 1 or General Staff 1. It presented itself as a station run by dissidents who were totally pro-German, and even pro-Hitler, but who deeply opposed the corruption and incompetence of the Nazi Party. Although transmitting from England, the station claimed to be operating from secret locations within the German Reich.

How did GS1 sound so convincing? First, all the key broadcasters were native Germans, many of them anti-Nazi former prisoners who knew German military slang and routines. Their news items came directly from intercepted radio broadcasts that Nazi officials sent to German newspapers. GS1 also rebroadcast speeches by Hitler and other leaders, tapped from actual German broadcasts. But GS1 put a subtle, and masterful, spin on these news items. For example, one story explained that Nazi leaders were worried that shortages would arise during the coming winter if too many citizens cashed in their clothing coupons. GS1 aired this item as a scandal story, explaining that wives of top Nazi officials were being tipped off to buy their new winter coats to avoid the shortages of warm clothing that would afflict German soldiers.

GS1 was so effective that the Americans, who did not know the secret at the time, recorded broadcasts to show that dissident groups were operating inside Nazi Germany. The British then set up two fake German services' broadcasting stations — Atlantiksender (for the U-boat service) and Soldatensender Calais (for the army). Both were accepted as genuine, so the British could transmit carefully written news items that hurt morale.

Even when the ruse was uncovered, the stations run by the Allies continued to damage morale, but in a different way. Fed with intelligence information from agents throughout the occupied countries, they could sprinkle their broadcasts with very accurate details. For example, it was devastating for a U-boat crew, setting off into a perilous Atlantic battle, where survival depended on remaining undetected, to hear the latest football scores from their own base, coupled with a record request for a named member of their crew. Such broadcasts could dash their hopes of returning safely and cripple their performance.

ABOVE William Joyce, popularly known as "Lord Haw Haw" because of his drawling delivery when making German propaganda broadcasts to Britain during World War II, under arrest in 1945.

AIRBORNE INTELLIGENCE

From the earliest experiments using balloons, airborne observation has given people new ways to gather intelligence.

When World War I broke out, both sides used balloons to spy from the air. However, they soon realized that powered aircraft could cover much larger areas on a single mission. At first, these aircraft carried trained men who reported what they

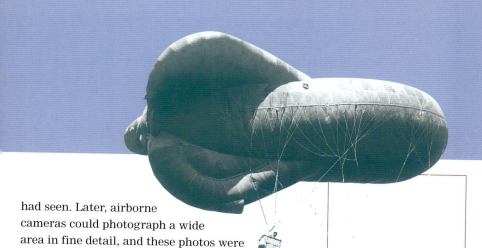

had seen. Later, airborne cameras could photograph a wide area in fine detail, and these photos were analyzed for any useful information.

Gradually the science of photo-interpretation was developed to make the most of aerial reconnaissance material. Trench warfare still dominated the battlefield, and photos could show details of enemy defenses. Fuel and ammunition dumps could show that the enemy was preparing to attack, while photos taken from a height of several thousand feet could show large groups of marching men.

To Hide the Truth — Camouflage

To combat the eye in the sky and mislead the enemy, the science of camouflage was developed. Gun emplacements were concealed by foliage or netting and buildings were coated with camouflage paint. Men could hide in trenches and underground bunkers, but vehicle tracks were harder to hide. Both sides also knew that they must survey the same sites repeatedly, since changes in the picture could help them detect even carefully hidden troop movements and supply concentrations.

By World War II, a wide range of military reconnaissance aircraft could provide even more data. Pictures of towns and cities might reveal industrial resources that would become attractive military targets. Photographs of airfields showed the strength and organization of defenses that bombers could attack. And when the raids were done, photos could determine whether they had succeeded.

ABOVE A World War I French observation balloon spotting for the artillery at Madenay on the Marne, July 6, 1917.

OPPOSITE Professor Thaddeus Lowe's observation balloon "Eagle" in the American Civil War, seen during a storm, with infantry, artillery and supply wagons in the background.

ABOVE German defensive positions near Westkapelle on the Dutch island of Walcheren, showing zigzag lines of trenches.

In one case, the military used photographic intelligence to revamp an entire campaign — the RAF Bomber Command's night bombing offensive against the heart of Nazi Germany. Neutral observers claimed that many heavy raids seemed to be missing their targets, while the bomber crews reported widespread damage. To find out the truth, the RAF fitted cameras to every bomber. Each camera was triggered by a flash flare, which was fired when the bombs were dropped, revealing the aircraft's exact location at that precise moment.

The resulting information was both valuable and discouraging. It showed that only a handful of bombers were striking anywhere near their targets, despite their crews' courage and devotion. The problems of navigating to Germany over a totally blacked-out Europe kept them from being certain of their position to within a few miles. Bomber Command responded to this crisis by developing new navigational techniques. The most experienced crews were used to relay information on winds and courses to less skilled companions. And in the longer term, radar-based navigation systems — like Gee, Oboe and H2S — were developed. They could guide bombers precisely to their targets despite thick clouds and poor visibility.

World War II Airborne Intelligence

During World War II, photo-reconnaissance techniques made great advances. New high-performance Allied aircraft could fly fast missions into the heart of Europe, take pictures and return without succumbing to enemy fighters or anti-aircraft fire. Some high-altitude missions covered a large area in a single pass. Others flew at treetop level to snap close-ups of specific sites. These low-level flights might occur at dawn or dusk, when the sun was low in the sky, casting long shadows on the ground that revealed much detail about the true shapes of objects being photographed.

Multiple, power-driven cameras could shoot a series of exposures on a single high-speed pass over a target, enabling "stereo pairs" to be produced. Photo-interpreters aligned adjacent prints taken on successive exposures and studied them through a stereoscopic viewer to see a detailed three-dimensional image. They could then see crucial facts like the heights of objects and even the shapes hidden under camouflage netting.

Amazing new systems made it even easier to see through camouflage schemes. Infra-red false color film reacted to the different temperature levels in the scene exposed to the camera. It could distinguish between dead and living foliage, so plants that had been cut and laid over a tank, truck or gun position stood out from the living landscape. Grass and plants that had been crushed were also revealed, to show where troops and vehicles had been hidden. And live soldiers gave off the most obvious signals of all, compared with dummies.

After World War II, new airborne reconnaissance systems gave even greater coverage of the ground

BELOW Camouflage sheeting and other concealment measures are intended to break up the outlines of factories and similar vulnerable targets so that they fail to show up in reconnaissance photos.

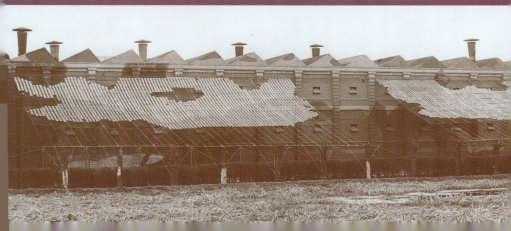

below. Infrared line scan systems could show target areas clearly at night and in poor visibility, building up quite a detailed picture. Aircraft with engines running could be clearly distinguished from dummies, or planes that were not running. Empty fuel storage tanks showed up differently than full tanks, and so on.

Radar coverage showed huge areas in less precise detail. For example, a high-flying jet could record a radar map of the whole Mediterranean in just two sorties. As in all these reconnaissance missions, regular coverage established patterns of ship movements, and so on. Changes in those patterns indicated possible dangers.

To combat high-performance aircraft and more powerful reconnaissance techniques, more formidable anti-aircraft defenses in the shape of surface-to-air missile (SAM) systems were developed. But even then, experts built reconnaissance planes that could evade these missile defenses.

Higher, Faster and Stealthier — the Rise of the Spyplane

The first specialized spyplane was the American Lockheed U2, developed in the 1950s. This was designed to fly at heights above 70,000 feet (21,000 m), to keep it safe from the fighters and anti-aircraft missiles of the time. Using the thinnest-possible sections of metal kept its weight to the minimum. Its basic design configuration was similar to that of a powered glider. In fact, once it had used its turbojet engine to climb to its operational height, the U2 would glide for long periods, ensuring maximum range and endurance.

The U2 entered service in 1956, carrying a new generation of special long-focus cameras. They were sighted through seven openings in the U2's skin to produce extremely detailed, high-quality pictures of a 125 mile–wide (200 km) strip of ground more than 10 miles (15 km) below. One test shot, taken from 55,000 feet (16,700 m), showed pictures of a golf

BELOW A U2 spyplane developed by Lockheed for covertly spying on the Soviet Union from 13 miles (20 km) up.

course. When these were enlarged, people could count the balls on one of the greens.

U2s flying from bases in Britain, Germany, Turkey, Pakistan and Japan could cover huge areas of the Soviet Union and bring back valuable pictures. In one series of missions, U2 photos of the Soviet aircraft industry showed that the Soviets did not have as much airpower as they wanted the West to believe.

In the end, the capture of Francis Gary Powers (see Case Study 15) showed that even the U2 was vulnerable to improved air defense systems. Although U2s could still deliver valuable information in more limited theaters of operation, nations sought new hi-tech designs to outwit the opposition.

One way of overcoming the defenses was with speed. Lockheed's SR71 Blackbird, which emerged in 1964, could soar higher than the U2 and could fly at up to three times the speed of sound. While the US ruled out long-distance overflights of the Soviet Union for political reasons, these aircraft could gather photographic and electronic information from other sensitive areas. Yet their height and speed protected them from hostile missiles and aircraft. Later designs, which combined shapes and surface finish to minimize radar reflections, would employ stealth as an alternative way to evade the enemy. However, by the time these sophisticated aircraft were introduced, satellites had become the main tool for airborne observation. They operated at heights far above those covered by the boundaries of national airspace regulations. Reconnaissance and intelligence-gathering had truly reached an exciting new dimension.

ABOVE A Lockheed SR71 Blackbird high-speed reconnaissance aircraft seen from a KC-135 tanker aircraft as it approaches the tanker's flight-refueling boom. When the two aircraft are close enough, one of the tanker's crew can steer the boom to make contact with the SR71's refueling point to replenish its tanks and extend its range.

HITLER'S REVENGE WEAPONS

EUROPE, 1943–44

During World War II, Allied intelligence began to hear disturbing reports that Hitler was building frightening new rocket weapons on a remote island off the Baltic coast, called Peenemünde. To confirm these reports, RAF photo-reconnaissance Spitfires went to the secret site. Their first photos showed that massive construction work had taken place for some highly technical activity. But in the photographs taken on June 12, 1943, a British intelligence expert spotted a silhouette of a large rocket lying on its side on a railroad flatcar. Clearly, this was a German rocket development center. Later missions produced pictures with even clearer views of rockets on the site.

In fact, these rockets were prototype V2s, the ballistic missiles that would be used against London, Paris and Antwerp. In an attempt to quash the threat, 597 RAF bombers were sent to bomb Peenemünde on the night of August 17/18, 1943. Although 41 aircraft were lost, the destruction severely delayed the rocket program.

In response, the Germans moved the later test and development program for the V2 to Occupied Poland, but Allied photo-reconnaissance discovered the switch. The long flatcars with their unmistakable cargoes were impossible to conceal and repeated RAF missions were able to track their movement from the Baltic coast to central Poland.

Nevertheless, other work continued around Peenemünde. Messages from agents, supported by clues in deciphered Enigma signals, showed that the Germans were also diligently working on a pilotless flying bomb, which they eventually called the V1. This was actually the world's first cruise missile.

Despite substantial evidence that the V1 existed, none had ever appeared in a photograph. But on November 28, 1943, an RAF photo-reconnaissance Mosquito flying over Zempin, close to Peenemünde, brought back prints showing the small silhouette of a V1. Close to each catapult installation at Peenemünde and Zempin was a strange long building with a curved end. These buildings were clearly linked with the V1 launch catapults. When air reconnaissance photographs of the Channel coast of northern France showed sites with similar buildings, they were made high-priority targets for Allied bombers and fighter-bombers. To launch this operation, 1,300 bombers of the US Eighth Air Force carried out a massive strike, dropping a total of 1,700 tons (1,730 t) of bombs.

Nevertheless, the V1 campaign against London began a week after D-Day, and 8,617 flying bombs had been fired before the advancing Allies pushed the Germans back out of range. Some 5,500 people died and 16,000 were seriously injured. However, without the dedicated work of the pilots and photo-interpreters who discovered the purpose and locations of the V1 sites, many more people would have died.

RIGHT The effects of a raid by Hitler's revenge weapons can be seen behind this fruit-stall in London.

OPPOSITE A V2 blasts off from a test stand at Peenemünde.

CAPTURED! FRANCIS GARY POWERS

US AND RUSSIA, 1960

After four years of fruitful flights over Soviet territory, the **U2** spyplane finally fell prey to air defense systems on **May 1, 1960**. At 6:26 a.m., a **U2** lifted off from a military airfield in **Pakistan** for the first south-north transit of the **Soviet Union**. This 3,800-mile (6,100 km) mission was intended to end in **Norway**. Its flightpath would carry it over **Afghanistan**, to monitor any space launches that might have been timed to coincide with the **May Day parade** in **Moscow**, then across the **Sverdlovsk industrial region** and the **Plesetsk missile test complex**. From there, it would cross the **Arctic coast of the Soviet Union** over the high-security naval and missile sites near **Murmansk**.

The mission began with some problems, including a 20-minute delay in the takeoff clearance and an intermittent fault in the autopilot. In previous weeks, the Soviets had protested these flights, backing up their complaints with accurate records of the routes across their territory. Clearly, Russian radar systems were tracking the aircraft. Furthermore, on earlier missions, pilots had occasionally seen fighters and anti-aircraft missiles trying, and failing, to reach their high altitudes. However, pilot Francis Gary Powers settled into the routine of following his precise flightpath as accurately as possible. He had passed the halfway point when the sudden impact of a Soviet anti-aircraft missile blew his world to pieces. His aircraft plunged into a steepening dive.

Powers struggled free of the wreckage and a barometric device opened his parachute automatically. Within minutes, he landed in open country, but was captured and taken to Moscow's Lubyanka prison. Three months later, he was tried as a spy and given a long prison sentence. Fragments of his plane were displayed in the capital and the Soviets exploited this valuable propaganda coup. They canceled a forthcoming summit meeting in Paris, between Soviet leader Nikita Khrushchev and President Eisenhower, and withdrew their invitation for the President to visit Russia. The relationship between the superpowers seemed to be deeply damaged.

ABOVE Gary Powers appears before the Senate Armed Services Committee in Washington, DC, with a model of a U2, following his exchange for Soviet spymaster Colonel Abel.

LEFT Powers listens to the indictment being read during the opening session of his trial in the Military Collegium of the USSR's Supreme Court.

OPPOSITE The wreckage of Powers' aircraft at the Gorki Park exhibition.

THE CUBAN MISSILE CRISIS

US, 1962

During the late summer of 1962, U2s from the US Air Force's Strategic Air Command, based at Laughlin Air Force Base in Texas, routinely flew over Cuba. Usually, the prints from these missions showed nothing particularly sensitive. But photos taken on August 29 showed new construction work at numerous sites — and these were clearly identified as surface-to-air missile (SAM) bases.

When the photographic interpreters checked material shot more than two years earlier over the Soviet Union, they found pictures that showed identical SAM sites protecting a ballistic missile launch site. Could the new bases in Cuba be meant for the same purpose? That situation would pose a deadly threat to the US.

Immediately, U2 flights over Cuba were doubled, but no trace of ballistic missiles was found. Yet agents operating within Cuba reported long cylindrical objects were arriving on Russian freighters. At last, on October 14 two more U2 missions brought back pictures that showed the Soviets were building the first ballistic missile launch complex on Cuban soil.

This was a critical moment in the shaky nuclear standoff between the two superpowers. The Kennedy administration ordered an all-out effort to find out the scope of the threat. By October 20, aircraft had

identified the positions and courses of over 2,000 ships in the Atlantic that might be sailing to Cuba. In the meantime, more U2 flights, along with low-level photo-reconnaissance missions by air force and naval aircraft, had found four ballistic missile sites under construction; 22 of the 24 SAM sites so far identified were operational.

On October 22, the President announced that if Russia launched any missile from Cuba against any nation in the western hemisphere, the US would regard this as a nuclear attack against them. They would then strike back on Soviet soil.

Five days later, a U2 was shot down by a SAM fired from Cuba. The world teetered on the brink of war, and US forces were placed on maximum alert. Then, Khruschev sent a message confirming that the missile sites on Cuba would be disassembled and the rockets would be returned to Russia. To provide confirmation, two US Air Force RF101 Voodoo reconnaissance planes were sent in on a low-level mission to photograph the missile sites. Dodging anti-aircraft fire, both crews completed their mission safely. The prints they brought back proved what everyone hoped to see: the missiles were being taken apart. Reconnaissance aircraft had helped to avoid the world's most dangerous crisis.

OPPOSITE
A Soviet merchant ship loaded with deck cargo, photographed by a US reconnaissance aircraft while on passage to Cuba in October 1962.

BELOW US photo-reconnaissance aircraft bring back more pictures of Cuban missile sites.

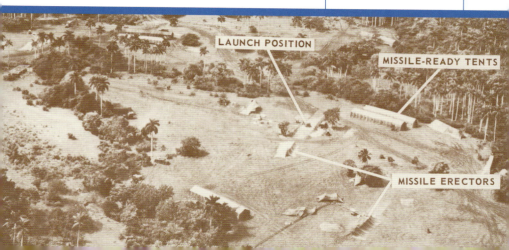

LAUNCH POSITION

MISSILE-READY TENTS

MISSILE ERECTORS

6

SATELLITES AND SPACE INTELLIGENCE

Aerial reconnaissance missions have always been steeped in danger. Planes spying on a country's military, industrial and communications resources may encounter bullets, shells and missiles, intended to keep them away. Faced with deadly fighters, anti-aircraft artillery and surface-to-air missiles, only the most skillful pilots reach their target and return to base with the valuable information that they seek.

International laws recognize a nation's authority over its airspace just as it has sovereignty over its land territory and coastal waters. Any unauthorized foreign aircraft that enters this space risks being driven off or being ordered to land. In extreme circumstances, they can be shot down.

Yet since October 1957, one country can examine another country's territory without risking retaliatory action. Intelligence-gathering changed forever when the Soviets launched *Sputnik 1*. This 184-pound (83 kg) satellite was blasted into space by a multi-stage rocket, which pushed it to a final speed of 18,000 miles (29,000 km) per hour. It orbited hundreds of miles above the earth, beyond any legal concepts of national airspace. *Sputnik* contained no array of cameras — only a miniature radio transmitter and batteries. But this was just the beginning.

Early Intelligence Satellites

Although the Soviet Union originally dominated the international space race, American satellites began to carry increasingly better instruments. And, as time went on, it became clear that satellites could do much more than just show off a nation's technological advances.

For example, early satellites tended to pass over most parts of the earth's surface in successive circuits. More powerful rockets sent them higher, giving them a wider "footprint," or area of coverage. Yet they were farther away from the surface. On the other hand, more accurate launch techniques enabled satellites to be placed in geosynchronous orbits. In these orbits, the speed of the satellite through space exactly matches the rotation of the earth below, so that it remains over the same spot on the surface. This meant satellites could be used as navigational beacons, communications relays, or early-warning devices to monitor certain types of activity, such as missile launches and similar sensitive events.

ABOVE Spy satellites provided top-quality pictures of territory that had not been covered previously, revealing information like the locations of military airfields, without the risk of attack by hostile aircraft or missiles.

OPPOSITE A *Cosmos* satellite is launched from the Plesetsk Cosmodrome in the Arkhangelsk region of Russia.

Cameras in the Sky

The US launched its first satellite after the Soviets but soon made up lost ground. On April 1, 1960, America sent a meteorological satellite named *Tiros-1* into an elliptical earth orbit. Powered by internal batteries, the 290-pound (130 kg) satellite contained two small TV cameras. They relayed their pictures directly to ground receiving stations when the satellite was in range. When out of range, it recorded them on tape, to be relayed later in its orbit.

Even these early cameras showed a clear view of airfields, missile sites and other defensive installations all over the world. Scientists developed satellites that provided even greater detail. On May 24, 1960, the US launched its first reconnaissance satellite. The *Midas* (for *Missile Defense Alarm System*) held sensitive infrared detectors that could pinpoint the plume of heat energy emitted when a ballistic missile was launched from earth.

Next came a program that used satellites in the *Discoverer* series, *Discoverer 13* being launched on August 10, 1960. These satellites used conventional cameras instead of electronic devices to produce pictures with finer resolution. In order to retrieve exposed film without bringing the satellite back to

earth, the satellite ejected a capsule of film in a container fitted with a parachute.

In August 1961, after a successful trial, *Discoverer 14* was launched with the full film and camera system. Its orbit took it over the entire Soviet Union. When the exposed film was recovered, the pictures showed airbases and rocket sites, although the resolution between 50 feet and 100 feet (15–30 m) was crude. A new age of espionage had begun.

The Missile Gap: Truth or Lie?

During 1961, *Discoverer* satellites showed the first Soviet ICBM (Intercontinental Ballistic Missiles) site and test facility in Russia. Additional flights gave more details, but their biggest feat was to disprove the so-called "missile gap." Western intelligence agencies had believed the Soviet Union had far more ballistic missiles deployed than the West, though they had no hard information to prove it. In reality, the frontline Soviet missile, the SS6, was large and heavy. It could only be moved on railroad flatcars or on big trucks that needed major high-quality highways. The satellite photos revealed all these transport links, without any evidence of missiles that matched Khruschev's chilling boasts.

Although America had closed the "satellite gap," the Russians rebounded with *Cosmos 4*. It was launched on April 26, 1962, in an orbit that covered the whole land area of the US. After three days, *Cosmos 4* returned to Earth with all the information it had been able to gather. More *Cosmos* satellites were launched during the next two years. They were sent into higher orbits than the US satellites, so they

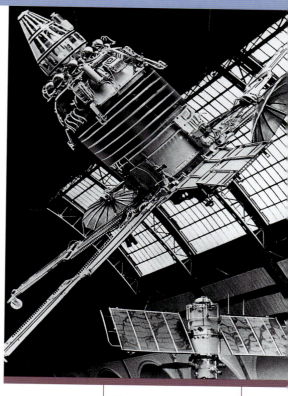

ABOVE A Soviet long-range intelligence-gathering satellite, *Molnija I,* assembled in the Space People's Economic Exhibition of 1967.

could stay aloft longer. But the higher orbits limited the resolution of the pictures.

The Americans then produced a series of satellites that monitored Soviet, Chinese and other air defense and missile control radars. The *Gambit* series of satellites was designed to switch from the broad coverage of the original photo-reconnaissance satellites to close-ups of specific areas.

Total Coverage — and New Hope for the Future

ABOVE A Soviet spy satellite based on the Soyus capsule.

At the end of 1963, the CIA reported that satellite coverage gave a clear view of most of the key military areas in the Soviet Union. Likewise, Soviet satellites were monitoring the key military sites of the US and Western allies. They could record details about missile systems, watch naval and military operations and monitor weapons testing. This meant that no nation could make a military strike without being noticed.

However, in case the unthinkable happened, the US developed the Minuteman concept to make sure some of the nation's missile resources could survive a surprise attack, and then strike back. They built far more launch sites than the number of missiles available, reasoning that Russia would have to hit every one to deliver a successful pre-emptive strike. Only some of the sites would contain missiles at any one time, but there was no way satellites could identify them. Besides, it was easier and cheaper to build launch sites than it was for the Soviets to build that same number of missiles.

However, as East and West negotiated arms-limitation and arms-reduction treaties, satellites served a more positive role. Earlier treaties had often stalled because it was difficult to make sure all the parties were complying with the conditions to everyone's satisfaction. Now satellites could monitor the changes from space. Once nations agreed to limits on missile deployment, anti-missile defense systems and conventional force levels, intelligence systems could help to end the arms race.

Star Wars

Satellites had a larger role than intelligence-gathering in the original Strategic Defense Initiative ballistic missile defense system (nicknamed "Star Wars") first proposed in the 1980s. First, they were to warn of the launch of hostile missiles. They would also carry many vital parts of the system, including lasers for destroying missiles and warheads and mirrors for directing the laser beams on to their targets. Scientists believed that lasers, which can carry a lot of energy, could move fast enough to hit incoming missiles and they believed the beams could be kept very narrowly focused over a long distance using mirrors.

Unfortunately, the system faced a major problem: scale. Modern ballistic missiles can split into a series of independently targeted warheads, so the defensive system would face tens of thousands of targets in a short space of time. The enemy might also use decoy warheads.

Also, the laser would have to be focused on the same spot on the skin of a fast-moving missile or warhead to burn through it. Hardening the missiles by adding heatshields, or simply spinning them in flight, would have greatly increased the time needed to achieve this. In addition, very large, high-quality mirrors would be required to focus the lasers. The tiniest imperfection could have made a mirror useless.

Furthermore, the mirrors would have had to survive being launched into orbit. Then they would need to maintain exactly the right attitude in space and withstand a laser beam powerful enough to destroy a missile. In all, more than 100 orbiting mirrors would have been needed to aim the laser beams. Finally, each laser would have had to be around 100 times more powerful than existing military lasers. The mirrors would have to be able to switch between targets accurately and instantly. The laser beams would have had to be perfectly aimed, and targeting decisions taken instantaneously. All these things added up to a formidable assignment, even for the world's most capable and sophisticated satellite specialists.

NUCLEAR EMERGENCY AT CHERNOBYL
US AND SOVIET UNION, 1985

Not all satellite missions involve military emergencies. On August 28, 1985, the US was launching a second KH11 satellite to replace one that had been brought down a month before. But shortly after the launch, the motors of the Titan rocket failed, and ground control had to destroy both the rocket and satellite before they could crash back down to earth. This disaster left only one KH11 in orbit. When the Americans attempted to launch a KH9 on April 18, 1986, this too failed.

As a result, the US had trouble responding immediately when an emergency occurred at the Chernobyl nuclear power plant, 80 miles (128 km) from Kiev in the Ukraine. Technicians at the plant practicing safety drills on April 26, 1986, had been using non-standard procedures that caused a runaway reaction. The reactor blew apart, releasing huge quantities of radioactive material into the atmosphere. The next day, an increase in communications traffic in the area suggested a crisis. One day later came the official Soviet statement.

Nuclear monitoring aircraft from Britain flew over Europe and the Mediterranean to measure the fallout, while the sole remaining KH11 was sent to check out the area later that same day. Its orbit at the time gave only a distant view, so little information was obtained. But the following day, April 29, the satellite took detailed pictures from directly over the reactor. The roof was missing and the walls had been blown out, leaving the interior a glowing mass of radioactive material.

OPPOSITE An aerial view of the wrecked reactor block at the Chernobyl nuclear power plant, which leaked a cloud of radioactive gas that spread across Europe in April 1986.

ABOVE Even today, years after the disaster, workers regularly check levels of radioactivity near the damaged reactor block at Chernobyl.

Further orbits of the KH11 monitored the cleanup operation, showing that the fire had been controlled. Helicopters were seen hovering overhead, dropping sacks of sand into the reactor interior to seal it off from the atmosphere. This was followed by tons of lead pellets to fill the gaps between the sacks and form a radioactive shield. Besides showing the cleanup, the satellite pictures also reassured people that the other Chernobyl reactors seemed unaffected by the catastrophe.

CRACKING THE GULF WAR SECRETS

US, 1990

On July 16, 1990, US satellites revealed the first signs of Saddam Hussein's coming invasion of Kuwait. Photos showed a brigade of Iraqi tanks occupying a previously empty area of desert near the Kuwaiti border. A day later, more tanks appeared, increasing the strength to two divisions; on July 18, a third armored division moved alongside them. The speed of this buildup set alarm bells ringing among the US intelligence community.

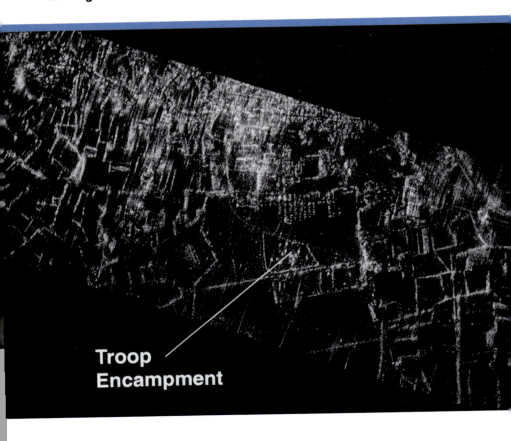

Troop Encampment

Ongoing satellite coverage showed the continuing military buildup, making it clear that a full-scale invasion would soon occur. By August 1, US intelligence predicted an attack within 24 hours. Iraqi troops proved that estimate correct as they crossed the border into Kuwait the morning of August 2, 1990.

As Western diplomats worked to gather a coalition of friendly forces in the region to pressure Iraq to withdraw, satellites played a key role. In addition to three orthodox KH11s, the US had an advanced KH11 with an infrared imaging capability to produce pictures at night. The Lacrosse radar–equipped satellite could produce less detailed images through cloud and in conditions of complete darkness.

Besides, specialized aircraft flying close to Iraqi airspace revealed details about Iraqi troop movements on the ground. At the same time, the Iraqis had no way to monitor the forces being assembled against them. They had no satellites, or access to satellite information, and the coalition fighters shot down their reconnaissance aircraft.

These resources gave coalition force commanders a priceless advantage over their Iraqi opponents when they began to liberate Kuwait in January 1991. Nevertheless, the situation revealed gaps in the satellites' coverage. With the end of the KH9 program, the new generation of satellites could not be kept over the area of the conflict longer than a short period each day. Ironically, a new problem came from the deadly accurate "smart" weapons that coalition air forces used against Iraqi buildings and installations. These bombs and missiles were designed to penetrate the outer walls and explode inside to cause maximum damage. Even high-precision satellites could "see" only the holes they made entering their targets but not the actual damage inflicted.

OPPOSITE US satellite imagery, showing evidence of Iraqi troop movements on the Kuwaiti border as a prelude to invasion, July **1990.**

BELOW The remains of a destroyed Iraqi tank lay abandoned in the desert.

7 ESPIONAGE IN THE TWENTY-FIRST CENTURY

The value of espionage seemed to peak in the twentieth century, as global wars and other conflicts caused more widespread terror and destruction than ever before. In earlier times, spies were useful, though they had less of an effect on the course of history. But the world wars of the 1900s threatened national survival. By digging out an enemy's secrets, and planting false information, intelligence services could determine who won the battle — and even the war.

RIGHT An artist's impression of the Aurora spyplane high in the atmosphere — believed by many sources to be a top-secret design to replace the extremely successful **US SR-71 Blackbird** surveillance aircraft.

OPPOSITE
US Secretary of State Colin Powell announcing the expulsion of five Russian Embassy officials, and stating that some 50 Russian intelligence officers using diplomatic cover would also have to leave the US.

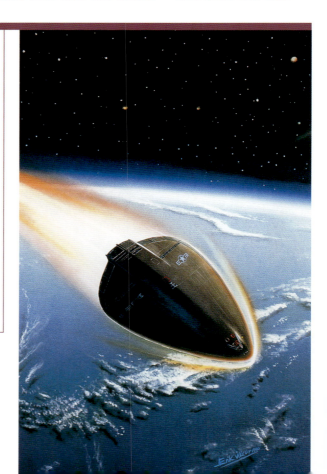

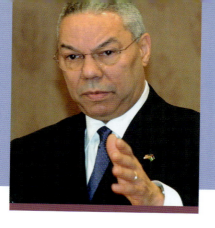

Furthermore, an uneasy peace followed 1945 as two superpowers built enough weapons to destroy all life on earth several times over. Besides the vital contributions made by brave, devoted human agents, new technologies can uncover an enemy's intentions and resources, and mislead them about one's own. Spyplanes and satellites, electronic and communications intelligence, traffic analysis and cipher-breaking and a range of other developments have made the espionage picture more complex and challenging than ever before.

The Cold War Ends

Ironically, these dramatic developments were occurring just as the old Cold War was ending. In a few short, but dramatic, years in the early 1990s, the awesome threat posed by the weaponry of the Soviet Union and its allies disappeared. The frontline units of the Russian Army withdrew from the Warsaw Pact countries hundreds of miles, taking them beyond the far borders of newly independent pieces of the Soviet state, like Belarus. Old Soviet republics, like the Ukraine, regained long-forgotten independence.

The world suddenly seemed much safer as the old secrecy vanished along with the Iron Curtain (the guarded border between the countries of the Soviet bloc and the rest of Europe). Now it was possible to talk to KGB agents and chiefs and to hear, firsthand, their view of espionage operations. In this new, more open climate, it seemed possible that espionage itself might become as dated as the barbed wire and minefields that had divided East and West Germany.

If that hope ever existed, it soon vanished. As the new century dawned, maybe the old threats were gone, but some suspicion remained between East and West, and their interests were not always the same. Russia feared the eastward expansion of NATO, as their former allies, like Hungary and Poland, sought to join that organization to protect them from any future revival of Russian power. Meanwhile, the West worried that newly democratic Russia might slide back into totalitarianism and militarism. Both sides had good reasons to keep a close watch on each other, so many Cold War agencies and networks continued as if nothing had changed.

New Links Between Old Foes

Early in 2001, in a scenario reminiscent of the 1940s and 1950s, the US ordered the expulsion of 50 Russian diplomats suspected of being espionage agents. This occurred after Vladimir Putin, a career KGB officer, became President of Russia, and espionage efforts became more important as the Russians fortified their Foreign Intelligence Agency, the SVR (Sluzhba Vneshney Razvedki).

Mass expulsions are serious business. In response, the target country usually deports the same number of the expelling country's representatives, both to retaliate and to suggest that both sides are guilty of covert activities. To risk harming US-Russian relations by such an action, which might also have compromised its own networks within Russia, the US must have thought national security was threatened.

Moreover, this expulsion was carried out against an extraordinary background. The SVR has regular, and often friendly, contacts with members of the CIA, and the two

BELOW Heavy security measures were put into place outside the Russian embassy in Washington DC following the expulsion of four suspected spies from the US on March 22, 2001.

services collaborate on areas of mutual interest, such as fighting international terrorism. Yet with its rising crime and declining economy, and a still mighty nuclear arsenal, Russia remains a major target for Western intelligence-gathering.

Challenges for New Technology

Besides the end of the Cold War, the biggest change in international espionage has been the rise of more states with nuclear and biological weapons which they can use to blackmail larger and more powerful countries. India and Pakistan have conducted successful nuclear tests and built more armaments. Iraq has a history of expelling UN weapons inspectors and concealing the level of its research and development of nuclear, chemical and biological weapons. At present, North Korea remains outside the influence of any power bloc. And China is an increasingly powerful and confident enigma to the global power structure.

BELOW Into the nuclear age: an Indian missile with nuclear warhead takes part in a military parade; both India and Pakistan have developed atomic weapons.

The latest technology raises hopes of keeping these multiple threats under close and continuous surveillance. Yet even the best modern satellites and sensors have their limits. During the Gulf War, the Iraqis tricked coalition aircraft into wasting missiles by setting up inflatable decoys fitted with heat sources to produce the right kind of signature to infrared target-seeking systems. The extensive satellite coverage of the war zone still could not pinpoint the Iraqis' mobile launchers for their Scud surface-to-surface missiles, which they

ABOVE Side Looking Infra Red (SLIR) port on an RAF Tornado GR.1A reconnaisance aircraft. Three of these give the aircraft horizon-to-horizon coverage.

fired at targets inside Israel.

On the other hand, the coalition effectively used radio-controlled pilotless drones, which drew the fire of the Iraqi air defense system, to confuse the enemy and drain its resources. This specialized use of drones represents a major step forward in intelligence-gathering over relatively small areas at low level, since they are small, cheap and expendable, and do not show up well on radar. They can loiter over a target area and send back visual, electronic or infrared information for a much longer period than any satellite.

The US has developed a hi-tech tiny robot, similar to a remote-controlled-car, that soldiers can send into buildings for reconnaissance to check for any potential dangers before they enter. It can sense radiation, biological hazards and chemical weapons and send this information back to a soldier at a remote location. This was used in Afghanistan to help search caves and bunkers. Hi-tech equipment such as this is slowly becoming a reality.

A Bright New Espionage World?

What lies ahead? Two advances mark the onset of the new century. The US is meeting the perceived threat from so-called rogue states by developing a new missile defense system to follow the "Star Wars" concept of the 1980s. Other nations have worried that this action might negate the existing Anti-Ballistic Missile Treaty, which prohibits defensive systems that could tilt the nuclear balance and destabilize the balance between East and West. In response, America proposed cutting its nuclear arsenal.

As of 2002, newspapers were reporting a new twist of this policy: they suggested that the defensive shield should use Russian S300 missiles, and that the two nations should hold joint exercises in identifying attacks with these missiles and successfully shooting them down. This could also involve the newer S400 missiles, together with related Russian radar systems. This proposal may not calm Russian fears, despite the financial benefits from the missile sales. Even more important, the Chinese are concerned that a successful anti-missile defense system cancels out the investments they have made on their ballistic missile capability.

ABOVE Signaller using frequency-hopping EW equipment to monitor enemy transmissions and then initiate automatic jamming equipment.

The second new US initiative is much less controversial, except on the grounds of cost. The $25 billion project called Future Image Architecture aims to produce many new spy satellites. These would be launched from 2005 onward to provide tighter coverage of the whole world. Their higher orbits will enable them to cover areas twice as long as existing satellites, using high-power optics, backed up by radar. They can then relay thousands of images, zooming in to areas of interest, in daylight, darkness or bad weather.

The CIA can take images from its latest satellites and process the information to create three-dimensional moving pictures of cities and military installations. Research is also being done on hyperspectral sensors, which could capture images from target objects using a combination of radar, ultraviolet and infrared sensors, along with conventional optical cameras. This would give many more details of the shape, density, temperature, chemical composition and movement of a target, and would also make it extremely hard to create a successful deception. In other words, hyperspectral sensors would show intelligence services whether "what they see" really is "what they get."

Certainly the future of intelligence looks exciting, but with so many political, technical and operational fronts, nobody can say for sure what lies ahead.

THE HO CHI MINH TRAIL

US, 1970s

During the Vietnam War, US forces needed to cut off supplies being sent to the Viet Cong in the south from the Communist north along the network of jungle tracks known as the Ho Chi Minh Trail. They could not send enough troops into the jungle to disrupt the flow of food, ammunition and reinforcements, so they decided to use heavy air strikes instead.

ABOVE US air squadron spraying a suspected Viet Cong position in the Vietnamese jungle with a defoliant liquid to deprive them of cover.

Good intelligence was vital to avoid wasting bombs and rockets. To obtain this information, aircraft were sent in to seed the whole Trail with huge quantities of remote sensors. Once these hit the ground or became caught up in the foliage, they became active. Some were sonic detectors that reacted to noise and movement; some were activated by vibration; and some were triggered by heat sources, or by the chemicals in human perspiration. A central computer system across the Thai border picked up the signals and analyzed where and when deliveries were being made. American fighter-bombers were sent in to drop huge quantities of napalm and high explosive in the area.

In the end, the campaign was only partially successful. This was because a vast number of different routes had to be covered and a large number of small groups, rather than substantial convoys, actually carried the supplies. As a result, large and worthwhile targets were rare. Also, the enemy found ways to locate, immobilize or deceive the sensors. Animals could trigger the sound and movement detectors, and even the perspiration sensors could be fooled by bags of human urine hung in the trees.

THE HANSSEN SPY CASE

US, 2001

Many spies have been driven by their ideology, hatred of a particular regime or the wish to make the world a better place by helping to shift the balance of power. Others are driven mostly, or entirely, by money — a trade that is proving more and more common.

ABOVE The charges against Hanssen carry the potential for the death penalty but his guilty plea had the sentence reduced to a true life sentence with no possibility of parole or early release.

Robert Hanssen was an FBI agent for 27 years. But in the most recent spy scandal to hit the US he has admitted that he worked as a Soviet agent since the mid-1980s for a vast payoff of cash and diamonds worth $1.4 million. Hanssen, who is only the third FBI officer to be accused of spying, apparently approached the Russians and offered them counterintelligence information in return for big payments.

Hanssen was very secretive. He preferred to use dead drops, and never met his Russian controllers face to face. Nevertheless, it appears that he passed 6,000 pages of sensitive information, including details of Russian double agents working for the Americans. As a result, at least three of them were recalled from the Soviet Embassy in Washington. In Moscow, they were interrogated. Two were executed, while the third was imprisoned.

Hanssen was arrested in early 2001, while leaving documents for his handlers at a dead letter drop in a suburban park in Virginia. Hoping to catch the Russians, the FBI kept watching that spot, but no one turned up to retrieve the valuable information. This led to fears that there were more double agents within the FBI. Maybe one of them could have warned the Russians? As a result, the FBI announced plans to increase the use of compulsory lie-detector tests for employees, and to restrict computer access.

THE ULTIMATE SECRET AGENT

Life as a secret agent is much easier with high-speed cars and gadgets that help to escape death at the last minute, spot enemies from far away and communicate easily with colleagues. How about a cigarette that carries a radio? A jacket that can take its owner soaring into the air? A dagger pen? Or an umbrella that turns into a gun? These are examples of the spy tools that appear in movies and television series.

BELOW Pierce Brosnan as James Bond in *Tomorrow Never Dies.*

The media have featured a dazzling array of high-tech gear that spies can use to carry out their daring work. Some of these gadgets really do exist, or they have been developed since they were shown on film. Often, the gadgets actually used by the CIA and other groups have been mysteries to the general public. Other gadgets have been invented to dazzle television and movie audiences and to make spy heroes and their adventures larger than life.

One of the best-known examples of a well-equipped spy is James Bond, the British super-agent created by author Ian Fleming. The first film featuring 007, as he is code-named, was released in the 1960s. In *From Russia With Love,* Bond had a pager before these came into general use. In the course of his movie career, Bond has chased Russian spies, dashed plots to ruin the global economy, located bombs and decoding machines and foiled terrorists.

Bond is often at his best behind the wheel. In every film, he has driven cars that can reach amazing speeds and foil pursuers by squirting water, creating a smokescreen, laying a coat of oil on the road or even launching a deadly missile. In *The Man with the Golden Gun,* Bond managed to escape by using a broken bridge to leap across a river. In *Diamonds Are Forever,* he drove his car on two wheels so he could maneuver into an alley. But these feats paled in comparison to the Lotus Esprit Bond drove in *The Spy Who Loved Me.* It could change from a land vehicle into a small submarine, equipped with sonar, a periscope and harpoon gun. Using a sidewinder on the "sub," Bond was able to attack a helicopter that was chasing him. The Bond cars are so resilient that they survive being rolled over or driven down steep hills or crashed into the cars of enemies.

In 1995, Bond began driving various versions of the German-made BMW. His car was fitted out with missiles located behind the headlights and tracking equipment that included all-points radar. Two years later, Bond appeared in *Tomorrow Never Dies* driving a BMW that contained armor and missiles and which could dispense tacks to shred the tires of anyone chasing him. This car also had a computer on board to facilitate Bond's communications. It could be driven by remote control. His BMW Z8, featured in *The World Is Not Enough*, could reach the 150 mph (240 km/h) mark. In the 2002 release *Die Another Day*, Bond's V-12 Vanquish Aston Martin was mounted with cameras and covered in a special cloaking system that allowed it to perfectly blend in with its surroundings, appearing invisible!

ABOVE One of 007's many spy gadgets. A security scrambler is cleverly disguised as a cell phone.

Bond carries special guns and other weapons to perform his various missions. But who needs a gun when you have a cigarette lighter that contains a tiny but very effective rocket? Or a cigarette case

ABOVE James Bond and Zao battle it out on the ice in their well-equipped Aston Martins in *Die Another Day*.

that holds poison-tipped darts? Inside one of Bond's wristwatches was a long, ultrathin steel wire that could be used to strangle opponents, a strong electro-magnet that could repel alligators and a miniature saw. Once, Bond's creative quartermaster, code-named "Q," designed a special exploding briefcase for 007. To avoid an untimely explosion, Bond had to turn the clasps a certain way if he wanted to open the briefcase for his own use.

What else keeps James Bond ahead of his competition? One of his cigarette lighters was really a device for reading microfilm. And along with his shaving kit, he packed a bug detector and signal sender in his suitcase in *Live and Let Die*. No less handy were the eyeglasses he wore in *A View To a Kill.* These enabled Bond to see into rooms that the human eye could not see on its own.

In turn, Bond has faced the creative and deadly tools used by his enemies. They have included powerful lasers, guns with special bullets and ranges, and music boxes containing high-tech communications gear. In one incident, Bond was the victim of a cigarette. When a beautiful female Russian spy took a puff, knockout gas was sent in Bond's direction. While he was out cold, she stole his microfilm. Needless to say, Bond used his ingenuity and spy tools to regain the microfilm and complete his mission.

THE WALKER SPY RING
USA, 1968–85

For the Russians, their greatest espionage coup against the Americans during the Cold War, surpassing even the network that gave Stalin the atomic bomb secrets, was the spy ring led by former US Navy officer John A. Walker Jr. He began spying in 1968, when he was serving as communications watch officer for the Atlantic Fleet submarine command in Norfolk, Virginia. With access to signals between US submarines in the Atlantic, Arctic and Mediterranean, he could pass on cipher keys and other technical information to his KGB controllers.

ABOVE John Walker (center), accused ringleader of the Walker spy ring, being led by police on his way to appear at the US District Court in Baltimore. Walker was expected to plead guilty to charges of passing US military secrets to the Russians.

As a result, the Russians made their own KL-47 cipher machine with the keys he had given them, to decipher US messages. Walker later served aboard two naval carriers, followed by a final tour at Atlantic Fleet Headquarters in Norfolk where he continued giving the KGB cipher keys and other information until he retired from the navy in 1976.

However, by then he had recruited Senior Chief Radioman Jerry Whitworth and Walker's brother, Arthur, and son, Michael. This group turned over a vast amount of material on ciphers, deception, electronic countermeasures, satellite communications systems and different types of weapons, together with operational textbooks. Michael gave details of highly secret weapons systems, including data on the Tomahawk cruise missile.

According to Soviet double agent Vitaly Yurchenko, Walker's information allowed the KGB to read more than a million secret US Navy communications. The network was betrayed when Walker's former wife alerted the FBI. In May 1985, Jerry Whitworth and John and Arthur Walker were given life sentences. Michael Walker was sentenced to 25 years in prison.

8

SPYING ON THE TERRORISTS

As the Cold War fades into history, Western intelligence and espionage services face the mounting threat of international terrorism. Terrorism tops the list of forces that can weaken major powers all over the world. Western intelligence agencies faced a daunting new challenge following the terrible events in the US on September 11, 2001. That morning, hijacked civilian airliners full of passengers were deliberately crashed into the World Trade Center and the Pentagon, killing thousands and injuring many others.

Since the 1980s, antiterrorism has become a heavy intelligence task. Spies and especially double agents who can penetrate these dangerous and secretive organizations offer the best hope of uncovering their plans in time to set up counter-measures. Some of these operations are conducted in foreign territory. In recent years, as global terrorists move into the territories of their targets, spies now operate inside their own countries, but surrounded by an alien immigrant religious or political faction.

Piercing the Terrorists' Web

To combat counter-terrorist operations, most successful terrorist organizations have adopted security measures used by intelligence services and the wartime resistance movements. They reduce the damage caused when an individual is identified or captured by dividing large groups into small cells and keeping contact to a minimum. They also take the utmost care in recruiting newcomers, to limit the chances of counter-terrorist double agents. Swift and terrible punishment of any person suspected of betrayal keeps others in line.

ABOVE Aerial view of Ground Zero — the base of the World Trade Center twin towers, in New York City, showing the destruction of the towers and adjacent buildings.

As a result, counter-terrorist groups must carefully recruit volunteers from within the same nationality, population, religious or political group as the terrorists themselves. This opens up the possibility that a double agent may turn out to be a triple agent, if the person they recruit is actually working with the terrorists. Counter-terrorist information could then be passed to those against whom it is targeted. In cases where agents are truly working for the counter-terrorist service that runs them, they face grave danger just by entering the terrorist community. Even if they are recruited, they may only come in contact with individuals in their own cell, at a low level in operational terms. Attempts to learn more details could make the real terrorists suspicious.

Some networks, particularly Middle Eastern ones, often use suicide and car bomb attack methods, and numerous terrorists accept death in making such attacks. These included the truck bombs against the US embassies in Nairobi and Dar-es-Salaam in 1998 and the suicide attack against the USS *Cole* in Aden harbour in 2000.

Security services are looking for effective ways to counter suicide attacks. So far, the responses have been mainly defensive. When Osama bin Laden's agents attacked US embassies in East Africa, the US closed down most embassies world-wide until it could see whether or not more attacks were coming. Assassinations are also difficult to counter when the assassins are willing to die with their victims, as happened with President Sadat of Egypt, whom fanatics hated for his role in helping to improve chances for peace in the Middle East, and Prime Minister Rabin in Israel for similar motives from the other side of the Arab-Israeli divide, and Prime Ministers Indira and Rajiv Gandhi in India.

OPPOSITE Many people required first aid when a truck bomb detonated below the World Trade Center in 1993, killing six people and injuring 1,000 others.

BELOW The new US embassy in Nairobi, built following the 1998 bombing.

Counter-Terrorism Successes

Counter-terrorism can succeed, however. Americans tracked down the men who made the first attempt to blow up the World Trade Center towers in 1993. On February 23, a yellow Ryder van containing a large bomb was parked in the underground garage below the North Tower. The plotters hoped the explosion would cause that tower to collapse against the second tower, bringing both down to kill tens or even hundreds of thousands of people. When detonated, the huge charge of 1,200 pounds (540 kg) of explosive killed six people and injured more than a thousand, causing more than (US)$500 million worth of damage.

The FBI mounted a massive investigation to catch the culprits. Soon, clues began to emerge. Like the recent and much deadlier attack, this effort involved numerous terrorist organizations, including probably bin Laden. They sought to destroy what they viewed as a symbol of the American-dominated global trade system and to punish the US for supporting Israel. Their planning was so careful that intelligence services had little or no advance warning.

Yet, in other ways, the conspirators were quite inept. One of them, Mohammad Salameh, returned to the Ryder rental office to claim the $400 deposit he had paid when he rented the van. He claimed the van had been stolen by Ramizi Ahmed Yousef, one of the bomb-making team, the day before the

blast. FBI agents traced leads back to a Jersey City apartment and a nearby storage shed used as a bomb-making factory. Inside, they found the fingerprints of the two men and another conspirator, Eyad Izmoil.

Both Yousef and Izmoil fled to the Middle East right after the bombing. But the long arm of the intelligence agencies pursued them, aided by a $2 million reward for information leading to their

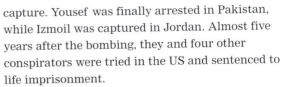

capture. Yousef was finally arrested in Pakistan, while Izmoil was captured in Jordan. Almost five years after the bombing, they and four other conspirators were tried in the US and sentenced to life imprisonment.

In another success, the Oklahoma bomber Timothy McVeigh was caught and convicted. McVeigh placed a bomb aboard a Ryder rental truck, then parked it in the basement car park of the Alfred P Murrah Federal Building in Oklahoma City on April 19, 1995. The resulting explosion killed 168 people, many of them young children attending a day-care center in the building.

Investigators traced part of a truck axle to a 1993 Ford truck rented from a Ryder office in Kansas. Employees described McVeigh and the artist's composite sketches were distributed to stations, hotels and restaurants between Junction City and Oklahoma City. McVeigh was identified by a manager at a hotel in Junction City. Agents discovered he was already in police custody, having been arrested for carrying a semiautomatic pistol. Forensic evidence showed traces of explosives on McVeigh's clothes, and empty barrels at the Michigan address on his driver's licence were very similar to fragments found at the bomb site. McVeigh was eventually executed.

More recently, the basis for Islamic terror groups has shifted, from the Shi'a Muslims, who were supported by Iran, to the much more numerous Sunni Muslims, who represent the vast majority of Muslims. Terrorists operate within the Muslim countries of Algeria, Indonesia, Pakistan, Saudi Arabia and Central Asia. Nations that appear to be sponsoring terrorism include Sudan, Syria, Lebanon, Iran (though this is now officially denied) and Afghanistan. Outside the Muslim world, there are other

BELOW A handcuffed Timothy McVeigh is escorted from the Noble County courthouse after originally being taken into custody for carrying an illegal semiautomatic pistol.

powerful terrorist organizations, some with rational political philosophies, others without.

Terrorism on a Global Scale

In recent years, terrorist organizations have used the large-scale movements of asylum seekers and the freedom and openness of Western society to expand. The many migrants to America and Europe from nations like Egypt, Iraq, Iran, Pakistan or Afghanistan include a small proportion of agents from the different terror networks. They have used their host countries as bases for recruitment, supply and funding for their operations within their target nations.

Fortunately for intelligence agents, as terror networks become increasingly global, there are more potential ways to uncover them. For example, agents of the right culture and background may find it easier to penetrate a network operating in a Western society than one hiding in the Afghan mountains or Iranian deserts. Next, and even more importantly, widely dispersed terror networks face more complex communications problems. Much of their publicity and recruitment information is now sent over the Internet. This enables intelligence services to learn more about the links and structures of these shadowy groups. Spy satellites that eavesdrop on microwave links and telephone conversations have picked up gems of information, like Osama bin Laden's instructions to his networks to go to ground in Afghanistan before the September 11 operation.

ABOVE Members of a specialist anti-gas chemical warfare unit of the Japanese Army check out a train in a Tokyo subway station following the 1995 sarin gas attack.

Obstacles to Counter-Terrorism

How can intelligence services fight these threats at home as well as in the most remote regions? Agents need courage, dedication and specialized expertise to

ABOVE A fighter for the Taliban Islamic regime in Afghanistan, regarded as a major harbor for terrorist groups, stationed near the front line against the Northern Alliance troops.

penetrate these highly motivated, ultra-religious groups. Potential agents need training in the cultural background of the groups they plan to infiltrate, including complete fluency in the colloquial speech and dialects of minority languages.

Yet the CIA in particular has faced formidable problems in placing agents into the terrorist networks that pose the most direct threat to the West. The Agency has lacked officers who can speak fluent Arabic or possess the appearance and background to pose as a member of bin Laden's network. Those who do have the necessary qualifications may be unwilling to spend months living in the Afghan mountains compared with the more hospitable and less remote terrorist centers like the West Bank and the Gaza Strip.

Legal issues pose other problems. Government regulations put in place in 1995 have discouraged the CIA from recruiting undercover sources of information within terrorist networks. These regulations allow intelligence officers to be held personally responsible for any illegal acts or human rights violations carried out by agents they recruited. In addition, the Justice Department has tended to refuse permission for telephone tapping to be carried out on suspected terror groups because of possible human rights violations.

A further limitation on CIA action was the ban on political assassinations, in place since 1976. The Clinton administration then introduced a blanket ban on recruiting any agents or even informers who had criminal records or had committed human rights violations. Nevertheless, details have emerged of an attempt to assassinate Osama bin Laden, which President Clinton originally backed in 1998, but the project was overtaken by events in Pakistan.

Fighting Tomorrow's Terrorist

Besides trying to place their own agents into terror networks, Western intelligence agencies may have to work with agencies in other countries that are geographically or culturally close to the nations that harbor them. One example is Pakistan. The Pakistani Inter Services Intelligence Agency (ISI) is based in Islamabad, where 100 officers run a network of agents operating within Afghanistan.

In the meantime, since 1998, and the attacks on the US embassies in Africa by bin Laden's al-Qaeda network, presidential directives imposed new rules of engagement on CIA agents in the field. The ban on attempting to assassinate a foreign head of state remained, but agents were allowed to use lethal force in self-defense. In practice, this meant terrorists could be killed immediately before they mounted an attack.

Though the CIA will not comment, other sources claim that, in collaboration with foreign intelligence agencies, agents have been able to prevent attacks by al-Qaeda in Kenya, Egypt, Jordan and in Europe. Spies and intelligence agents continue trying to pinpoint accurately the whereabouts of the terrorist chiefs in order to launch military attacks designed to eliminate the threat those chiefs present.

ABOVE A soldier of the Afghan Taliban movement firing artillery north of Kabul.

THE LOCKERBIE DISASTER

SCOTLAND, 1988

A notorious terrorist crime against civilians took place on December 21, 1988. A Pan American Boeing 747 flying from London to New York was crossing over south-western Scotland at its cruising height of 31,000 feet (9,500 m), when a bomb in the hold of the aircraft was set off. As the huge 747 broke up, the nose section was torn away and the airliner fell upon the small town of Lockerbie. All 243 passengers on board were killed, with another 11 victims on the ground.

BELOW The baggage container which had held the bomb painstakingly reassembled as part of the reconstruction of the airliner and its contents.

Investigators resolved to track down the killers. They traced more than four million pieces of wreckage collected over nearly 1,000 square miles (2,600 km^2). In order to explain the order of its break-up, the pieces had to be put together to reconstruct nine-tenths of the aircraft. Experts found tiny bomb fragments, with traces of Semtex explosive, trapped in the skin of the plane's luggage compartment, along with clothing fibers and fragments of a brown suitcase. Further tests showed the case had been transferred from a Frankfurt flight.

At that time, a terrorist would know that security checks at Frankfurt were less strict than in London. Bags that had been

checked there would not be checked again when transferred to the New York flight. Furthermore, a passenger could accompany bags on the Frankfurt-London sector and not board the New York flight.

Previous intelligence reports had also indicated that a major terrorist action could occur during this time. Intelligence agents had warned that terrorist groups were intending to put plastic explosives inside electronic equipment in unaccompanied baggage. The CIA had received a specific warning on December 5 that a Finnish woman would place a bomb aboard a Pan American flight from Frankfurt.

Clothing fiber evidence from Lockerbie included a garment with a label from a clothing manufacturer in Malta, an island with close ties to Libya. The trail led to a store, where staff remembered a man of Arabic appearance buying clothes that closely resembled the fragments found at the explosion site. Furthermore, airline baggage records showed that a bag from Frankfurt placed aboard the 747 had originally been sent from Malta. Intelligence agencies also knew that when the attack occurred, Abu Taib, a senior member of the Popular Front for the Liberation of Palestine, was actually in Malta.

The puzzle came together as investigators traced the Semtex explosive to Libya, and positively identified the man who bought the clothes in Malta as one of the Libyans later accused of the crime. Experts concluded that this attack was mounted in revenge for an earlier US bombing attack on Libya in retaliation for a Libyan-backed terrorist raid against US forces in Germany. After intense diplomatic pressure and severe economic sanctions, Libya released the two suspects so they could stand trial. At a special Scottish court set up in Holland, one of them, Abdel Basset Ali Megrahi, was finally convicted, almost 13 years after the disaster.

ABOVE Libyan agents Al Amin Khalifa Fhima and Abdel Basset Ali Megrahi were eventually put on trial for the bombing.

OSAMA BIN LADEN
US, 1990s–2001

One of the world's most notorious terrorists is Osama bin Laden. He developed his militant views while fighting as a volunteer in Afghanistan against the invading Soviet forces, where his units were actually aided by the CIA. He switched targets in 1991 when he objected to American forces remaining within Saudi borders after the Gulf War. They stayed to help deter further Iraqi exploits. But bin Laden claimed the Americans' real purpose was a crusade against Islam.

As time passed, his views and his actions grew more extreme. In 1996, he declared a "jihad," or holy war, against Americans in Saudi Arabia. Bombs in American barracks were followed by attacks further afield in Somalia and, most bloodily, in East Africa.

The 1998 attacks followed a second declaration of war against Americans and their allies, civilians or military, anywhere in the world. Bin Laden's followers detonated two huge truck bombs outside the American embassies in Nairobi in Kenya and in Dar es Salaam in Tanzania, killing 224 people. In October 2000 a suicide bomber in a small craft loaded with explosive rammed the American destroyer USS *Cole* in Aden harbour. Finally, in September 2001, his hatred for America resulted in the destruction of the World Trade Center in New York City and the loss of thousands of innocent lives.

Bin Laden is an intelligence agent's nightmare. He has mounted disinformation and deception campaigns against the US by using decoy teams and sending false messages over communications channels monitored by Western intelligence. US intelligence has followed bin Laden's satellite telephone conversations since 1996. However, more recently his

ABOVE Islamic fundamentalist and terrorist chief Osama bin Laden, leader of the al-Qaeda group held responsible for the attacks on the World Trade Center and the Pentagon in September 2001 in addition to the US embassy attacks in 1998.

al-Qaeda network switched to sending messages by couriers carrying coded instructions to be relayed from telephones in Pakistan. At one point, there was a rumor that he was visiting a training camp in eastern Afghanistan after the Embassy bombings to meet leaders of other terrorist groups. The US Navy fired 70 cruise missiles at the area, only to find bin Laden had already left the camp.

Another time, the Americans thought he was based in a complex of mountain caves in eastern Afghanistan. After the US strikes, he may have moved to a new base in the Pamir Mountains, traveling in darkness in convoys of black all-terrain vehicles, escorted by Arab volunteers. Even with topnotch satellite surveillance and signal intelligence, intelligence agents face huge problems locating a target in such a remote area.

In 1998, President Clinton authorized US intelligence services to try and capture or assassinate bin Laden. The following July, squads of special services commandoes went to the remote Parachinar camp in North Pakistan, close to the Afghan border, for training. Pakistan's Prime Minister, Nawaz Sharif, and the Pakistan Inter Services Intelligence Agency were collaborating with the American squads to provide retired intelligence agents as guides to find bin Laden. The mission was almost ready to depart when Nawaz Sharif was deposed in the coup that brought a new leader, General Musharraf, to power. The project was abandoned.

BELOW
US Marines search a series of tunnels discovered in Kandahar, Afghanistan.

Abwehr the German intelligence service from the 1920s until 1944.

Agent a person, usually a foreign national, who has been recruited by an intelligence service to perform concealed missions.

Asset a clandestine source or method, usually an agent.

Audio surveillance operation a clandestine eavesdropping procedure usually with electronic devices.

Black operations clandestine or covert operations not attributable to the organization involved.

Cheka Russian secret police founded in 1917 to serve the Bolshevik Party; one of the many forerunners of the KGB.

CIA the Central Intelligence Agency of the United States of America, formed in 1947 to conduct foreign intelligence collection and counter intelligence operations.

Cipher a code where numbers or letters are systematically substituted for open text.

Clandestine operation an intelligence operation designed to remain secret as long as possible.

Code a system used to obscure a message by use of a cipher or by using a mark, symbol, sound or any innocuous verse or piece of music.

COMINT communications intelligence usually gathered by technical interception and code-breaking but also by use of human agents and surreptitious entry.

Concealment device any one of a variety of devices used to secretly store and transport materials relating to an operation.

Controller often used interchangeably with handler but usually means a hostile force is involved, that is the agent has come under control of the opposition.

Dead drop a secret location where materials can be left concealed for another party to retrieve. This eliminates the need for real time contact in hostile situations.

Defector a person who has intelligence value who, volunteers to work for another intelligence service. They may be requesting asylum or can remain in place.

Double agent an agent who has come under the control of another intelligence service and is being used against his original handlers.

ELINT electronic intelligence usually collected by technical interception such as telemetry from a rocket launch collected at a distance.

Handler a case officer who is responsible for handling an agent in an operation.

Hostile (service, surveillance, etc.) term used to describe the organizations and activities of the enemy "opposition services."

HUMINT human intelligence, collected by human sources, such as agents.

Infiltration (operation) secretly or covertly moving an operative into a target area with the idea that their presence will go undetected for the appropriate amount of time.

KGB all-powerful intelligence and security service of the USSR during the Cold War. Successor of Cheka.

MI5 the British domestic counterintelligence service.

MI6 the British foreign intelligence service.

Microdot a photographic reduction of a message, so small it can be hidden in plain sight or buried, for example, under the period at the end of this sentence.

Mole a human penetration into an intelligence service or other highly sensitive organization. Quite often a mole is a defector who agrees to work in place.

Mossad Israel's foreign intelligence service.

NKVD Soviet security and intelligence organization 1934–1946.

Okhrana secret police organization under the Russian Czars 1881–1917.

One-time pad (OTP) sheets of paper or silk printed with random five-number group ciphers to be used to encode and decode messages.

Pattern the behavior and daily routine of an operative who makes his own unique identity.

Personal meeting a clandestine meeting between two operatives, always the most desirable but more risky form of communication.

PHOTINT photographic intelligence; renamed IMINT, image intelligence. Usually involving high-altitude reconnaissance using spy satellites or aircraft.

Index

Picture Credits

The publisher would like to thank the following for permission to reproduce images. While every effort has been made to ensure this listing is correct, the publisher apologizes for any omissions.

AKG London: 4, 15-t+b, 16, 17, 21, 24, 25, 32, 35, 36-r, 37-l,r+c, 38, 44-tl+b, 45, 47, 51, 64, 65, 67, 70-bl, 74, 95. **AKG/Eric Lessing:** 14-b, 36-t. **Associated Press/Topham:** 26, 29-t+b, 31-b. **Culver:** 7 and back cover. **David King Collection:** 12, 13-t. **Eric Vicktor/Science Photo Library:** 1, 102. **Frank Spooner Pictures/Gamma:** 22, 23. **Getty Images:** 6, 10, 28, 34-b, 52, 53, 54, 58, 63, 68, 69, 79, 87, 90, 91, 103, 104, 109, 115, 117, 118, 120, 123-t, 124. **Getty Images/AFP:** 98, 116. **Getty Images/Marina Jefferson:** front cover-top. **Getty Images/Time Life Pictures:** 14, 18, 27, 53-t, 55, 62, 84, 88, 94, 113, 119, 123-b. **Imperial War Museum:** 19, 48-tl, 49-t, 50, 51-b, 66-b, 70-tl, 71-b, 72-b, 80, 81, 82. **Jean-Lop-Charmet/Science Photo Library:** 39. **Kobal:** 111. **MPL International:** 93, 100. **Novosti:** 92. **PA Photos:** 46, 99, 105, 106-t, 107-t. **Public Record Office:** 5, 33-tr and front cover, 40 and front cover, 42, 71-tr, 72-t, 73, 76, 77-t+b, 79, 82-b, 56. **Science and Society Photo Library:** 2, 20, 33, 35, 43, 85-tr. **Topham:** 110 and front cover, 112, 125. **Topham/Associated Press:** 11-tr and front cover. **Topham Picturepoint:** 7-tl, 8, 9-t, 11-bl, 14, 30, 31, 66-tl, 86, 89, 96, 101, 108. **US Navy:** 60-61.